DAYS LIKE THIS ARE NECESSARY

NEW & SELECTED POEMS

DAYS LIKE THIS ARE NECESSARY

NEW & SELECTED POEMS

WALTER BARGEN
FIRST POET LAUREATE OF MISSOURI

FOREWORD BY KEVIN PRUFER
ART BY MIKE SLEADD

BkMk Press
University of Missouri-Kansas City

BkMk Press
University of Missouri-Kansas City
5101 Rockhill Road
Kansas City, Missouri 64110
(816) 235-2558 (voice) / (816) 235-2611 (fax)
www.umkc.edu/bkmk

MAC
MISSOURI ARTS COUNCIL

Financial assistance for this project has been provided by the Missouri Arts
Council, a state agency.

Cover & section page art: Mike Sleadd
Author photo: Taylor Galscock
Book interior design: Susan L. Schurman
Managing editor: Ben Furnish

BkMk Press wishes to thank Elizabeth Gromling, Karen I. Johnson,
Molly Lesher, Melissa Lytton, and Kate Meadows.

Printing by Walsworth Publishing, Marceline, Missouri

Library of Congress Cataloging-in-Publication Data

Bargen, Walter.
  Days like this are necessary : new and selected poems / Walter Bargen.
    p. cm.
  ISBN 978-1-886157-70-5 (pbk. : alk. paper)
  I. Title.
  PS3552.A6162D39 2009
  811'.54--dc22
                        2009015749

This book is set in Palatino and Perpetua Titling MT.

Acknowledgments

Many of the poems in this book previously appeared in the books *Theban Traffic, Remedies for Vertigo* (Cherry Grove Collections); *West of West, The Body of Water, Harmonic Balance, Water Breathing Air, Vertical River, Rising Waters, Yet Other Waters* (Timberline Press); *The Feast, At the Dead Center of Day, Mysteries in the Public Domain* (BkMk Press); and *Fields of Thenar* (K. M. Gentile), as well as in the following publications:

American Letters & Commentary
Beloit Poetry Journal
Big Muddy
Black Rock & Sage
Chariton Review
Chester H. Jones Foundation Anthology
Delmar
Denver Quarterly
Farmer's Market
Fathers Anthology/St. Martin's Press
Icarus Press Anthology
In the Teeth of the Wind
July Fourth Press Anthology
Kansas Quarterly
Laurel Review
Melicreview.com
Mid-American Review
Missouri Review
Montserrat Review
New Letters
Permafrost
Pleiades
Poetry Salzburg Review
Prairie Schooner
Quarter After Eight
River Styx
Slant
South Dakota Review
Southern Indiana Review
Sow's Ear Poetry Review
2Rivers View
War Poetry/Winning Writers
Webster Review
Willow Springs

DAYS LIKE THIS ARE NECESSARY

THEBAN TRAFFIC

THE FEAST

FIELDS OF THENAR

MYSTERIES IN THE PUBLIC DOMAIN

HARMONIC BALANCE

BODY OF WATER
from *Yet Other Waters*

from *The Vertical River*

from *Water Breathing Air*

REMEDIES FOR VERTIGO

WEST OF WEST

Foreword

Walter Bargen is the author of thirteen critically acclaimed books and his poems appear widely in major national journals. He's won the William Rockhill Nelson Award for the best poetry book by a Missouri or Kansas poet and a National Endowment for the Arts Fellowship. Twice he's been the recipient of the Stanley Hanks Memorial Award from the St. Louis Poetry Center (and is, because of this, ineligible to win again). He's also quite possibly the most energetic community advocate for poetry that Missouri has ever seen. For as long as I've known him—nearly two decades now—he's run one literary reading series or another, hosting probably hundreds of poets. He interviews poets on the radio and, as Missouri's first Poet Laureate, travels the state giving readings, speaking to school children, talking about the value and power of poetry on television, judging poetry competitions. And finally, and most importantly, Walter Bargen is a tremendously talented writer. His work is technically sophisticated, rhythmically subtle, and emotionally complex, but—and here's the trick—it's also the kind of poetry that one might offer to someone who says he doesn't like poetry all that much, someone who claims he doesn't "get" poetry, someone who prefers mysteries or history books or biographies. It has always seemed to me that one of Walter Bargen's great gifts is his ability to speak directly to any intelligent reader, without compromising in any way, and to make himself understood, in all his complexity.

Not that there's anything particularly wrong with difficult poetry, poetry one has to wrestle with, poetry that assumes a background in one literary movement or another as a prerequisite to comprehension—but that's just not Walter's style. He'd rather his poems sidle up to the reader and engage him in pleasant conversation, say, perhaps, "here's a story you haven't heard before," then go on to tell it with skill and intelligence and thoughtfulness. His voice is not the rarified voice of the muse, nor is it the elusive voice of the academic. It is the voice of the neighbor or the friend from the office, and in his poems one senses always a highly intelligent mind finding in the everyday—in the fields or streets, in the news of the world—a source of meaning and truth. (Not that he isn't also prone to flights of surrealism—in his book *The*

Feast, a modern-day Jonah narrates many of the poems from within the belly of fish who has swallowed him—but even at his most whimsical, Bargen is also straightforward, seeming to tell us, "here I am, and here's another story for you.")

So why, then, when I cross the border out of Missouri, when I am in, say, Illinois or Ohio or Connecticut, do serious readers shake their heads in ignorance when I mention Walter's work? Sure, they're interested in reading it, they say, but it's just never come their way.

Some of this may have to do with the fact that Walter is no academic and, therefore, not part of that Byzantine network of university-based poetry readings traversed 10,000 times a year by our many poet professors, good and bad. Or perhaps he's not exactly writing in any of the modes of poetry that are stylish today—that is, he doesn't associate himself with any particular poetic "school" or style, nor does he see the world through the lens of any predominating literary theory.

And perhaps Walter Bargen's work, for all its ambition, grace, and skill, has been unfairly painted with the brush of regionalism. His voice, after all, has the characteristics many readers associate with the Midwest—that is, he's deceptively plainspoken and he often writes about the people and things one might see in Ashland, Missouri. But these traits—and they are traits more than they are representative of any particular regional aesthetic, if such a thing even exists—should not keep Walter Bargen's very fine poetry from those readers who will certainly find in it a source of great enjoyment and enlightenment. And for this, I am grateful for the publication of this omnibus volume of Walter Bargen's work, a volume that covers the entire career of one of the Midwest's very finest writers. In a perfect world, this book will go a long way toward bringing Walter Bargen's poetry to the much wider audience it deserves.

—Kevin Prufer

AT PLAY IN THE RUINS

DAYS LIKE THIS ARE NECESSARY
11/01/03

Fifteen men, the beginning of a pirate's song,
and the dead man's chest, a premonition, a prophecy,
a treasure too dark to be opened alive.
Disregard that they are called soldiers
dressed in combat fatigues, crowded
into the body of a helicopter, their weapons
on safety a bad joke. They've been given leave,
are being ferried to an airport, away from
skirmishes, frontlines, that are every street,
alley, roof, door, window, and at that moment
when the whump, whump, whump of turning blades
is the air's homing heartbeat, a harvesting scythe,
the helicopter missiled, is a flaming meteor,
scattering fifteen men across a desert,
others mangled in ways we are never told
but know, as in the song fifteen men
on a dead man's chest and a bottle of rum.

An Asian ladybug whirs onto my shoulder.
I'm surprised to hear the dim dental drill
of its wings so late in the year, and how it clings
to my plaid shirt. I carefully remove it,
send it on its way, an infestation
I can't battle, can't win, and live with,
accepting, admiring their tenacity.
It's unseasonably warm, wind from the south.
The crows are mewing like cats. Jays crowd
a dead elm, shrieking in defiance.
Small birds twitter their way through
the underbrush finding what's overlooked.
Leaves are falling casualties.
Shards of sunlight mark their down turning.
Days like this are necessary.

LOVE OF COUNTRY

So much familiar. A hand-sized effigy:
the fleshy clay of modest breasts,
ample belly, recessed navel,
rounded face, hairless mound of Venus.
Her hands bound behind her,
legs folded back, feet tied.
Each palm, each foot, both eyes
and ears, solar plexus,
crown of head, vagina,
anus, each pierced with an inch-long spine.

The erotic enemy,
the body torched and whipped
by desire: *attract, inflame, destroy,*
burn . . .until she leaps forth
and comes. . . out of passion
and love, in this very hour, immediately,
immediately, quickly, quickly.
So spoke Apalos to Karosa
in Eshmunen, Egypt, two millennia ago.

It is Sarapammon of Antinoopolis
who commissioned this clay woman
to invoke the gods and a dead man's
spirit to enamor Ptolemais.
She is to be bound by magic,
to be tortured by her lust until there is
respite but with him, unrequited,
love's effigy burning through countries of time.

ZOONOTIC

Caged, toothless, a lion sits in the manner of Kabul
alley cats, front paws slightly curled inward
toward his chest, hind legs folded close to his body,
head erect, staring beyond what moves beyond the bars.
Marjan's mane mangled from a grenade,
five years ago his mate killed.
He'd mauled the victorious fighter who'd entered
his enclosure to celebrate, lion to lion.
He survives revenge and today's war,
gunfire, guided bombs. Near starvation,
he gums the flank of something tossed to him.
Alley cats steal in to steal choice pieces.
From neglect, old age, he dies.

Ten years earlier, Kuwait City evacuated,
desert-hued walls shrapnel-riddled,
hippos, big as burnt-out Mercedes,
wandered the streets. Sharks, more or less lucky,
pulled from algae-festering aquariums,
barbequed by the invading army.
A confused giraffe stared into
a flashing traffic light. Cages opened,
toucan and parrots perched on bullets.
At the city limits, steel-latticed stems
of a hundred desert derricks
sabotaged into unfurling black blooms.

Half-a-century earlier,
by order of the Japanese army,
at the Ueno Zoo in Tokyo,
shortly before the flash and ash
of Hiroshima and Nagasaki,
the cages left open, tigers, leopards,
bears, snakes, all poisoned.

Three elephants, John, Tonky, and Wanly,
wouldn't eat the poisoned potatoes.
Syringe needles too weak
to pierce their skins. Seventeen days later,
John starved to death. Tonky and Wanly,
weak and thin, lifted their bony bodies,
stood on their hind legs, raising
their trunks as high,
performing their bonsai trick,
begging for food, for water.
No one said a word. No one said
their trainer went mad giving
them what they needed.
Everyone prayed for one more day
and tomorrow the bombing would end.
Two weeks later, they died, trunks stretched,
hooked high between the bars of their cage.

If that prayed-for time exists,
perhaps my father found it,
mowing the lawn, raking leaves,
finishing the basement with cheap
wood paneling, washing and waxing
a series of cars, a shine maintained
between wars. My mother kept
some of the bowling trophies,
emptied the closets of his clothes,
gave away all the shoes except
his German dance clogs,
the ones with a military spit-shine.
I kept the patches, the chevrons,
insignias, medals, flags,
the photographs. His leather belts,
I could wrap around me twice.
One cut of gray, wrinkled
elephant skin, stamped *Echt Leder*.

FACING A WALL

1

Hallway light dim.
Two men face the wall,
noses nearly touching the map,
its corners slightly torn by pins.
Hands try to smooth
the tectonic upthrust of creases.
They stare under their raised glasses,
their foreheads another set
of glazed-over eyes. "Vacation?
It would be a great place.
All these countries within
a few hundred miles
of each other." Only a raven
would think this. A few thin blue veins
trace roads, not all the blood
that has led here.

2

High desert, declivities, depressions,
oddities of geography: an arm, appendix,
archipelago, a reach of land that follows
a valley farther than it should where the Panj River
joins with the short run of the Pamir
from its headwaters at Sorkol Lake
in the Wakhan Mountains.
Hundreds of miles later, near the city
of Abjag, or maybe earlier where the Valchsh River
merges, the Panj is gathered into the Amu Darya.
Across the Garagum Desert and the Turan

Lowlands, near Taxiatosh it begins
to slow down, break into sluggish wet strands,
and in the middle of Qoraqalpog'iston
it is a vast swamp. The waters
of the Amu Darya never reach the Aral Sea.
Below pale fingers a thousand-mile-long river
disappears. Maybe it runs in the other direction
and they retrace the twisting blue line
back to the Panj. From one country
into another maybe it's called the Murghob.

REFIGURATIONS

1

Not even the sound of one hand
after she finishes speaking.
The audience's stares amputated
from their faces. Wrenched
out of their seats, they remain seated.
The shells of their ears burned open.
Deep in the meat of their bodies
they hear—from the bottom
of their pockets and purses, the space
between sock and shoe, something
that will never shake free of their
tweeds and blouses. It will be there
on the drive home, and later
after cocktails, the tiramisu will
ooze in a way they've never noticed.
For now she sits quietly
on stage, in the glare that details
the reconstruction of a flare-flamed life.
She is beyond friendship.
She remains in her room.
In front of hundreds,
she remains behind the door
of her skin and the topography
of heat: cracked, melted,
fused into a face.

2

Even after the girl who sits politely
with one leg crossed over the other,
print dress ending at her knees,
in her lap rests a pair of flesh-colored
plastic feet, so tranquil, as if they just
returned from a stroll through fallen
leaves, having kicked up a trail,
feeling the earth turning cool
and dormant, seeing a turtle back
its shell into the mud of hibernation,
a frog slow in its leap from the creek
bank, as if the water were no longer
a hiding place. These smooth-molded
feet like a purse with toes, resting
in the folds of her dress, open below
the ankles, the holes waiting for her
to drop in the small change of her
life, long after the blades swept past,
the audience hears the dull impact:
thunk, thunk, thunk,
the targets deep in their seats,
they see her hemline and what touches
the floor, a space made for feet.

FLAGGING

Outside the single-story school,
wind-swept prairie
has flagpole cables
beating a metallic martial rhythm.
The full-faced flag
stretches for a glory it can't know.
Some day it will hang limp.
Exhausted, we grow limp,
call it flagging.

We are called to believe more,
to make sacrifices: God,
family, blood drive.
After work, I enter the school gymnasium.
From clear plastic backboards,
hoops hang from heavens of victory,
but it's always too short
for any and all of our lives.
It's the day to day
that finally
outdistances us.

The questionnaire: malaria,
hepatitis, AIDS, the common current cold.
Not this time, but I check too quickly.
The nurse, in cowboy boots, makes corrections
to my mistaken diseases.
The blood drive sponsored by my daughter's class.
I've taken iron supplements
bought to counter the thin gruel
in my veins.
A daughter wants to donate
the blood of a father.

The nurse asks the next set of questions
as if I might not believe in sex

with other men, with prostitutes,
or needled street-drug visions.

I'm ready for the quick,
decisive prick. No wet bead
bubbles at my fingertip.
My skin turns alabaster,
a finger that Michelangelo
hammered, sanded, polished
out of dolomite.
The blood has flowed backward
into the rock.
This is a hand beyond even a sculptor's touch.
She squeezes, and what remains hidden,
a red fable–not enough
to fill the thinnest pipette.
She asks me to squeeze
what no longer belongs to me.

The nurse asks if I'm OK.
I tell her yes, though this finger
could belong to her. I say yes again.
No lights flash.
No spurs jangle. No cheers from
the folded bleachers.

I'm staring from another life,
seated in the chair across from her.
She's still holding
my hand.   I passed out.
No, I passed away.
I'm grieving, what slipped beyond—
the unfettered, unconscious,
so effortless, unlike this one.

I'm ready to give blood. I don't tell her
I feel terrible,
having to come back
to a pricked body. How perfectly
peaceful those seconds slouched
in a hard wooden chair
beyond knowing, though I couldn't
know until afterward.

She deposits me, where my daughter
waits, at the dessert table
festooned with tiny flags
where all the pale veterans sit,
flagging and fainted alike.

HARD ACT, 1969

The only light in the house from the open
refrigerator door. Kitchen chair and table
iron shadows. An hour before dawn,
I'm packing food in a torn grocery bag.

I step into a star-washed night.
Blurred by sleep, I follow headlights
to an abandoned house south of town.
Century oaks surround weathered walls

and busted out windows. The front door
fallen to the porch, one splintered edge
a dam for last year's rotting leaves.
I walk over the door into the house.

Shout. Two young men my age step
out of a closet. They dig through the bag
with the enthusiasm of children.
We crawl out a window practicing escape.

The yard simmers with sunrise.
They face off in foot-long, Hendrix-fringed
leather. Jackets quake a wake with each turn.
Jeans stained from a week of fugitive wear.

Red bandanas tied around necks, hair storms
faces, clouding shoulders, lips hidden
behind mustache and beards.
Twenty feet apart, arms slightly bowed

away from thin bodies, hands cocked,
ready to pull pearled six-shooters
from ornately sewn holsters—the sun
boils above the horizon. They stare at the targets

they've become. Jack-rabbit quickness,
they shoot each other, mouthing explosive reports,

index fingers smoking. Backwards, both
somersault, landing hard on booted heels,

fringe shivering seconds,
the drugs real, the war fantasy.

M-I-A

I chose the synthetic short-haired wig
to match my hair color,
a flooded muddy river.
I bought it in a costume shop
on a side street downtown
after my first interview.

The room was long, narrow,
cramped with four old men.
The draft board, all WW II vets,
convinced I'm cannon fodder.
Interview perfunctory, appeal anticipated,
they threatened to sheep-shear
my shoulder length hair.

Hours before the second interview,
I brushed my hair, used bobby pins
to flatten uneven strands,
lifted the wig out of a plastic bag
like something half-dead,
fluffed it, pulled it down
like a heavy curtain closing
to an empty house. When I entered
the room, they wanted to search
me for a tape recorder. The interview
quickly over. After a lifetime
of combat, surrender.

Decades later, in Phoenix, Seattle,
Denver, in motels and airports,
waiting for the next connection,
I flip through phone books,
running my index finger down
the long columns of names.
They aren't there. Or I've forgotten
the exact spelling.

SKINNED MAP

Last fall's fields a sorry mess of shattered stalks
and shotgun shells. Horizons of mayhem—
gutted, wind-ravaged clouds

bellying over hedgeapple windbreaks.
Somber-suited they work the furrows,
the corn crutches of another hobbled season.

Heads down, monkish crows
methodical in their march along the rows,
dark notes scored to a muddy dirge.

Deep-cleated tractor tracks mark
the composer's orphaned signature.
A desolate chorus, blackened birds

lacerate late February air.
They pluck feathers for Euripides
and Sophocles, for the fallen Trojans,

the Spartans at Thermopylae.
Their crank cries feed our torments
as another man dies under our skins.

TWO O'CLOCK ALL AROUND THE WAR

Fog off-burns into sun-hard blinding.
We squint, hold up hands for shade,
some confuse it for a salute,
see what is expected and move ahead anyway,
the point already behind us.

——— ——— ———

Shadows whipped to cowering.
A beached, black-masted season
of shipwrecked skeletons.
Marooned, dark outlines buck up
and down over the glass sea
of the window. Fleets of snow
and submarine rain rot the sash.
A dirt-stained pane loosens:
rattles: falls: breaks:
stiletto shards defy melting.
Oblique lakes of light
frozen over the floor
work their way toward the door
fingered with blood.

——— ——— ———

Each room abandoned,
each hallway leads to its own end.
Bedrooms submerged deeper
into induced numbness. The houses
that don't burn,
aren't bulldozed,
drift apart into futures of empty cupboards.
Deep undercurrents undercut foundations.
Roofs drift. Doors sail open.

——— ——— ———

A thousand-mile light, bass suspended in
a wet glass paperweight, between the sun's fiery upheaval

and a weed-choked bottom. Yellow-fringed
lilies float in air above lush circular pads
wide as elephant's feet, their green steps cross the water.

Cattails half surround the pond. Long-bladed leaves
wave over their martial reflections.
Nearby fields pour down bleached dry grasses.
Tufts of broomsedge flame in late light.
Crickets keep the hard machinery of song
marching toward night. Main street,
small town invested in slow decline,
the new store sign, The Turtle Club, pictures a bend
in the river where the restless drink to their bottoms
reminiscing this or that war.

——— —— ——

In Vedic text, the earth rides the back of four elephants.
If one elephant breaks a leg, shakes a leg,
is on a last leg, discovers it doesn't have a leg to stand
on, there's still enough to support a wobbling planet
as the herd teeters on the back of a turtle swimming the
void.

——— —— ——

Children were not the first to invent the slow plotting
beast
of the future, sitting at the table, staring at a plate
of uneaten greens. Sitting. The turtle shell rattle,
sewn closed with hide, filled with the rhythm of seeds,
the rolling, rhythmic rain, one that can't be escaped,
no matter how brutally we distract each other, no
matter the many and the matter exploding around us.

THE PASEO
—for Federico Garcia Lorca

The last flung-back, bullet-struck
moment on an arid Andalsian slope
of the Spanish Civil War;
a soldier's death caught
in shades of black and white,
his body halfway falling back forever
toward his shadow, his rifle pointed
at heaven, his head turned away,
already forgetting to tell us the way.
A woman's gaunt upturned face,
lips drawn back from her teeth, a forehead
of plowed wrinkles, her eyes straining
to find the sewing-machine hidden
in the sky, clouds being stitched
together with threads of fear,
and we know what happened,
the dusty, dive-bombed rubble
of Barcelona, the child at the slope
of her exposed breast
nursing on oblivion.

In the city where I lived one summer
oaks rose in civil explosions of leaves.
Branches arbored the boulevards
over the speeding cars and trucks
that had somewhere more important
in mind, work or love, not the quaking
heart of an air raid siren. Mostly it was Friday,
maybe Saturday evenings, that I drove
the Paseo as it was called, the body of asphalt
releasing the day's mesmerizing heat.
Along the way, fountains reared horses
and breached dolphins, spouting a moist
eternal glitter, surrounded by groomed

green esplanades where I might stroll
an equally endless time. In one
breath *paseo* simply means ride,
and in a different one it means
take him for a ride, the end of one
language and the beginning of another.

THE INVENTION OF FLIGHT

The windows are closed.
The glass smudged
with breath.   It's late winter
or early spring. The forward seats
of the passenger car
are occupied by soldiers.
It could be the beginning
of another war when victory
is believable, or the middle
when there is still hope.

In the railroad station,
I climb steps,
entering a high darkness
and feel my way to an empty seat.
I carry a delicate wire cage draped
in a blanket. I hold it high
so it doesn't drag.

Their braggadocio crowded
with foreign names.
Smoke from cigarettes
spins through dim lighting.
I can't really see them
except for their campaign hats
draped over back rests.
Each story followed
by the clink of flasks.
Hats are thrown into
the air, but I'm too young
and tired to listen.

I lie on my side across two seats,
curl my legs around
the cage behind my knees.
A small high-pitched singing

stops all the joking; a bird's song,
out of place, out of this world.
Faces hollowed with shadows
look up and down the aisle.
The train rocks, rattles as the hulk
of a passing freight smears the window.

BERLIN AIRLIFT

Between the right hand and the left a plan,
a reason for throwing stones at the sand
castle at the other end of the sandbox.
Kids lined up in two opposing rows,
facing off, grabbing what we can on a Saturday
morning, overthrowing this world,
betting victory on our aims.

A tower falls to the first stone, a drawbridge
collapses to a jabbed stick, the moat chocks
with crumbling walls; we shout explosions
and death cries. The devastation incomplete,
we search for more ammunition. One night
during those years I awoke past midnight,
sitting up, shouting just those words,

"More ammunition," until I was panting
from somewhere in the heat of dreaming,
from defending a losing position,
stormed by a life I would later surrender to.
By the sandbox, the battle in the balance,
I bent to pick up a fist-sized stone,
my head too clearly there in front,

and I felt the sharp impact. That was all,
and I didn't bother to throw anything else
or look for what it was that rocked my head,
not in an up-and-down yes or a pivoting back
and forth no, but side to side, as if saying
something between, acknowledging what wasn't
supposed to be there. I turned away,

walked across the playground, considering
my luck and how I was warned earlier not
to throw stones. I turned the corner
of the apartment building, met a grade-school
friend, who screamed, who shrieked at meeting
the walking wounded on a day nearly forgotten,
between wars, under the drone of cargo planes.

END OF THE ROPE

This is not a vision of hundreds of kids
straining hand over hand toward heaven
and getting tangled in the rafters.
Not a vision of a house built

from the roof down. My legs struggled
to wrap around the two-inch thick rope
to brake a too rapid descent, palms
and inner thighs hemp-burned.

None of us destined for the angels
but a cheap-street high. I didn't care
about beating the clock. Everyone else
in class faster. The coach an ex-drill sergeant.

We kids didn't know, didn't care, weren't listening,
we wanted to kill each other right then,
not in a future war. Years later,
the ropes still burn.

LOST ORDNANCE

The first shovelful alive and rich.
I'm down on my knees breaking clods
with my hands; cool and smeared
across my palms, clouding my fingernails,
a damp earth that knows its time.
Standing again, I drive the shovel's blade
with a boot, hit something hard:
a muffled ring. It happens a second time.

I begin carefully to dig, remembering
the mid-river sandbar one dry spring
on the Nekar a few years after the war.
Staring into rippled shocks of light,
I saw the black outline of a machine gun
exposed by the retreating water. Too young,
I couldn't swim the current to save it.

Those summers outside Heidelberg,
in the many-feet-thick fortifications
overgrown by sapling pines, it was there
I played my death over and over,
at one jagged blown hole or another,
on top of the parapet or in an empty
gun emplacement, my cheek finding
the carpet of moss, and somehow
my body jumping up to rehearse
the charge again. It didn't matter which
side I was on, the dying was so easy.
Around the perimeter, I dug
spent shell casings that had hardly aged,
arranging their calibers
along bullet-riddled concrete ledges.
I'd toss their dirt-packed shiny brass into the air,
the filth of battle dusting my clothes.

Not far, the groomed hills,
where one slope bowed into another,
as if they really did go on beyond
the entrance of white columns,
the fluted marble pillared against
a roof of engraved sky where words
fell one letter at a time on upturned eyes.
The surrounding flags streaked their colors
through wind, reminders of where
once they left and then arrived across
all those fields flowing with white crosses,
stars, and crescents, as if the most
important things we do are done over
and over. Holding my father's hand,
walking the perfect rows, looking for
no one name among the many, he was
surprised not to find his own–battle weary,
orders to hold his position fading.

On weekends I'd see through the rain-flecked
back window, fields of bomb craters turned
upside down in streaming lenses of rain.
Still the craters filled with water,
working themselves into weed-choked
ponds where frogs exploded into a new season.

Through Weinheim and Ludwigshofen,
couples in shorts and sandals strolled arm
in arm, behind baby carriages and dogs
straining leashes, as if it were normal
to pass buildings with just one wall standing,
rooms crowded with sky, under eaves
with corners gouged out, stone and bricks
scribbled with the graffiti of shrapnel.

I work the shovel slowly now,
an ocean, a continent of time away,
feeling for the hidden edges, wanting to
loosen without jarring, knowing
of grenades, lost ordnance, that missed

their wars, their seed slow to detonate
in others' gardens and backyards,
where other children play
at the dead center of day.

SNAPPED SHOTS

Two riveted holes elegantly threaded
with braided red string. *Grosse Buch,*
Hesse & Becker, Leipzig. Faded photo album.

Hundreds of dull, diamond-patterned ridges,
worn away at the corners.
Back cover stained, a mirage of coastline,

peninsula curving back into bay,
where an unnamed river enters the studded
cardboard-green sea. Miles from shore

the spreading oil from a torpedoed ship.
Above, the sputter of a B-17, the crew
thinking it safer to scatter themselves in the sea.

Small white paint spots, the trail of flak
following the bomber as it spins out of control,
and the parachutes of those still trying to return

to us after all these years. Turned over, the knot
in the red string flattened after half-a-century
of face-down-attic forgetting.

Where the stain wraps into a smudge,
the rubble of a city, the shadow of something shot
through, a dried pool at ground zero.

In the upper left hand corner, silver-embossed
wheat sheaves, their stalks cross the handle
of a red-rimmed spade, and on the blade

a broken-legged cross. Open, one young face
appears under field cap and helmet,
at attention, bespeckled, eyes pinched by small

round frames—always smiling—tossing a grenade,
baring the shoulder of a friend to expose
the pfennig-sized shrapnel scar, kneeling

in snow, rifle ready. This must've
been at the beginning, when it was easy
to believe anything invincible and manifest,

superior and godly. Platoon posed on dunes
by the North Sea, poised to launch rafts toward
double-spired churches impaling heaven;

in the drunken pose of a one-room party, a singing
that will be recalled in springs to come, the beaming
foolish faces of forgotten young men. The final photos:

smoke braided above blitzed tanks, a single
file of soldiers stretched toward the horizon,
drudging a muddy rut, backs turned

to a faceless fate. Somewhere a mother,
a father, an untameable grief,
who also might be face down

and indistinguishable in some field.
Once headed toward defeating the world,
half the album blank.

THE ELVES OF KATYN FOREST

It started during the night after the burning of many cities.
It started when the soldiers in uniforms the color of miles
of muddy road began the forced march of the defeated.
The mud of the vanquished and the mud of the victors

indistinguishable. Prisoners became guards, guards prisoners.
Dressed in fear and exhaustion, no one any longer cared.
It started in a faraway country, years before, when money
heaped in wheelbarrows was spent on a loaf of bread;

when someone in a palace signed his name in water;
when a cigarette butt on a sidewalk was punishable by conscription.
It started in a shirt pocket crowded with rats, in a bowl full
of glass eyes blinking in all directions in a field hospital.

So the long muddled lines drudged into a dark forest
to a strange mumbled cadence–the belch of boots being sucked in
and out of mired miles—forty-thousand struggling vowels
and rifle reports the only consonants spoken over the dead

guarding the ditches. Soon the forest turned blacker than
its wet pines. For years, the raw upturned earth burst
into small blooms of brass buttons and bones. An entire country
stopped breathing. Each year the trees grew more bloated.

A half century later, out of Katyn Forest miles of mud-caked
uniforms march. At dust-choked crossroads villagers look for
passing cars. The sucking sound, the faint moans, only wind twisting
through the gargoyled and steepled churches. Couples stroll along

rivers, watching their children run ahead. Cottonwoods sail their
leaves on the reddening current. The evening grows faint;
the sun's pulse weak on the water. The children shiver, listening
to stories of elves who return to retake the country they lost.

MILITARY SURPLUS, LEXINGTON, MO.

The Berlin Wall fell—
Kids standing on top, spotlighted
by guard towers, waving flags,
bearing body parts. The crowds
swelling by the hour. Hammers,
then sledges, then jack hammers,
then whatever heavy construction
equipment could make it
through the shoulder to shoulder,
shout against shout, song above song,
throng. I was just getting out of the army.
East Germany was a disaster.
You could buy anything. People were
desperate for money. I took my military
retirement and bought two entire Army
bases—lock, stock, and gun barrel for practically
nothing. Jeeps, tanks, warehouses full
of brand new uniforms, unopened crates
of Soviet weapons, explosives of every type.
What's left is what you see in this store:
gas masks, military caps, officer's epaulettes,
backpacks, boxes of medals, binoculars,
all stamped with hammer and sickle.
In the window, there's two dummies
dressed in camouflage, grenades hanging
from belts, plastic faces smeared black,
arms raised to attack through the dusty
afternoon light of the storefront glass.
So boring outfitting death in standard
issue and waiting for someone to pay.
Make me an offer.

AFTER WE DIE

I ask my mother for photos
of my father in the Korean War.
Yes, in the red album on the shelf in the closet.
She opens the door and asks would I mind
reaching it. The years have grown short,
the album over-sized and thick.
I'll return it on my next visit.

From first to last page, I see my mother
in her mid-twenties, wedding photographs,
bridesmaids smiling. What it must have meant
to marry into another country, to leave
a rubbled city, avenues blocked by burnt out trollies,
houses and gardens firestormed,
cities consecrated in human ashes,
but not a father's photos.

There's a small smiling, towheaded boy,
long eyelashes, grinning, who I wouldn't recognize
if it hadn't been pointed out, who I don't recognize
except to accept it's me. There's foggy Brussels
during the '58 World's Fair, when we slept
in a tent for three nights amid a city of tents
in the globular shadows of the Atomium.

Neuchatel by a mountain lake,
the guest house we lived in for six months
where I read French comics about two boys battling
the Axis powers, not understanding a word of French.
Then one photograph, the military cemetery: the crosses,
the crescents, the stars, their regimented rows
parading to the horizon. It's labeled Korea.

Four pages later, another military cemetery,
the crosses at attention, standard-issue,
identical to those previously pictured,
same angle on the mown hills,
shadows not an inch different—
it's labeled Liege, Belgium.
After we die, we die everywhere.

SNAKE ACT: THE MOVIE

"You certainly have a lovely baby."
"That's nothing. You should see his photograph."

Even if we don't believe L.A. burning,
and most of us don't after the attacks
of the killer tomatoes, the hand, the blob,
the soul-sucking pods, giant spiders,
cockroaches that spell threatening messages
on walls, and *Them*, the radiated ants; plus
the earthquakes, towering infernos, tidal waves,
hurricanes; and the possessed and demonic;
what's left? This first exalted day
of the living dead, I watch from under
the sonic slap of helicopter blades,
telephoto videotape of a driver wrenched
from his truck cab, thrown to the pavement,
fist in the face, foot in the face, a handful
of concrete to his brains, then up and spinning
on his feet, spewing the fireworks of blood–
in America life goes on, and for good measure
someone rolls him for his wallet.

> Below the porch three cats crowd around
> the knotted ribbon of a green snake,
> its pale belly turned up, and in their
> crouched conference they expect something
> more, but it's too late. I pick up
> the snake, not bothering to do anything
> else but lift the garbage lid. Its long
> thin body slides down the side
> of the plastic liner, escaping
> into the refuse of my life.

The looters in T-shirts and tennis shoes
crowd the store doors, leaving with boxes
hoisted on shoulders, chairs balanced
on backs, arms stretched to capacity,
having reached the unreachable.

They don't bother to hide their faces.
Some glance at camera crews,
some stop to be interviewed, it's their
turn to star in the material world,
lead roles in the redistribution;
but ask why—why not the stereo
and the jewelry? With pickups backed
to shattered windows, they strap down
stoves, refrigerators, televisions,
and drive off into the West of L.A.

> On the driveway I call to my daughter
> for the hoe, not wanting to lose sight
> of the coiled snake, tongue a forked
> flickering slash, a thin line of black fire.
> The copper bands are striking,
> and I don't hesitate—swinging,
> aiming for just behind the head,
> but missing. Something dark bulges
> and slides out from its scales as it battles
> the air. Something's wrong.
> Its underside is speckled and not deathly
> pale, its head not a jagged triangle,
> its pupils round with panic.
> It writhes in the hole I've dug
> and is out of sight with one shovelful.

The reporter backed against the storefront,
surrounded by four jacketed kids; he won't
give up the keys to his rental car. His only
way out of the burning; their way back.
His front teeth are bashed with the microphone
he carries, his nose broken with a left jab.
Down on his knees in that near final
position of not so foolishly embracing
a sidewalk, he hears the car engine start.

Eventually, we are all prisoners
of something; I've tapped my foot
to "Richard Cory" while living out
of dumpsters and sharing what seemed
a wasted wealth, proud case of expired
cottage cheese, bag of overripe avocados.
And it's not that my uncle had cared after
so many months high in the Carpathian
Mountains, where his legs began to feel
unnatural without skis, almost ready
to believe that his body was blue all
the way through, that his skin was meant
to burn and peel, as if he were cold-blooded,
patiently absorbed in the fierce calculations
of ambush; but finally even he recognized
the losses. He was captured in a white
uniform in a green forest, and because he led
brother against brother, he was taken to
a lumber mill and stood in a line that wrapped
around hills of rotting sawdust. The horse-
sized saw blade spit heads on the ground,
headless bodies stacked deep into wagons
until he was at the head of the line,
his camouflage already the color of blood
and mud, when artillery laid siege
and guards dove for cover under
the dripping wagons. His medals for valor
hang in a house that was once half barn,
chickens in the loft. He later returned
to the front, which was everywhere,
and was not heard from again. Life
is sooner and later, and I watched
from the attic window of the same house,
an old woman wring feathered necks—
on their breasts, their claws shoved
at the ground, on their backs,
their wings flapped.

The future of the past is always in doubt;
one war loses out to the next one, civil
disorders ordered and reasoned.
Out over the Pacific, beyond Marina
Del Rey, the pastels of evening float above
a horizon no one can reach, where scales
of light flicker off the sea's muscled blue,
where the deep on deep of water and sky
sets adrift the longing of watchers along
beaches, and the sun's electric threads
shimmer over the waves. Others walk
the docks to their boats moored
like empty souls, start engines, set sails,
leave wakes churning around log pilings
and dissolving behind jetties, leaving palms
alone to brush the breeze along boulevards.
They move beyond the rich traffic,
away from this great bowl of exhaust,
through a smoke-filled stage.
Just before earth's shadow pulls tight,
salt winds begin whipping across their backs.

> The other snake I didn't see, it's growing
> larger, swallowing a hawk, threatening
> to fly, to wrap itself around a reddening sky;
> then it's swallowing a fish, inexplicably panting
> on the lawn, walking like the creature
> from the Black Lagoon. I'm a thousand
> miles from any ocean. The cats have all
> run under the porch or into the house.
> A daughter holds open the screen door
> for their four-legged dash. From the field
> all I see is her arm and know by its ease
> she isn't aware of the danger. I'm left
> holding the hoe. The snake chokes down
> a tree. Its tail stretches across the county.

It's time to call for help: the police,
the army, Kong if he's still parked
on the back lot and not too rusty.

The present slithers out of the smoldering
to face the blowout. Years are gutted on
the editing floor and film strips sinew over
the edge of wastebaskets. The smoke of one
fire fades into a thousand, and the twisted
steel girders reach out of the rubble to threaten
the lenses. Shadows burn into the faces
of buildings: souls blackened and lost,
souls that can never again be reached,
Hiroshima's extinguished on La Segunda
Boulevard; and there on the grocery's wall
the stain of an execution. Rage is the only
ideology. It marches over a confetti of glass,
leading the feasts of flames, following
symphonies of smoke. Life goes on
or not, the cameras zoom in, pan back,
catch the ashes in tidal winds
that swarm the faces of cleanup crews.

LIFE DRAWINGS

... all truths are half-truths.
—A. N. Whitehead

In this ward are children
with missing feet, who hold up
drawings of missing feet, who tell us
one night they sat on the edge
of a great storm called history,
and they removed their shoes,
and their feet followed as they slipped
them under their beds. In the morning
they couldn't find them. They ask us
to please ignore the crutches; they are
practicing—it was always their desire
to walk on air. Looking closer, there are
rainbow-feathered wings sprouting
on the crayoned lines of their ankles.

The men in this ward are missing both arms,
and hold between their teeth drawings
of their arms. They have scratched
stick figures on their bleeding tongues.
They tell us they were not
common murderers, lurking in shadows,
stealing lives, but soldiers. One day
in an uproar of earth and buildings,
their arms flew off to perch in splintered
branches, on shattered window sills.
Now they can't hold their guns, embrace
a tree. We shake hands to feet in greetings.
They apologize for their dirty soles.

Down this corridor are the citizens
with missing heads, who balance
drawings of their heads on their necks.
They cut slits just under bushy-
penciled eyebrows fastened to pull tabs

to flutter their paper eyelids mascaraed
with red and silver sparkles.
They wink at our passing.
They understand what it's like to walk
through a forest of stumps
and hear, not the corridor fan turned
on to exhaust the overwhelming antiseptic
fumes, but the rustle of dry leaves
that are their paper-thin heads. They ask
forgiveness, for having thought less
of us, the thick-skulled ones,
who want to see it only our way.

WARRANT OFFICER OOSTERVEEN
REPORTS FROM THE SHOWER

In the shower he worries
over the next car payment,
what it is his son, his daughter,

really want from him. What was
intended by whatever wasn't worth
arguing but argued anyway.

A wet echo runs down the walls.
What little he speaks to himself is still
too much.   He looks down, chin to

chest, a refugee in his own bathroom.
His belly channels water. The old
blemish, a water drained

of evening light, his heart,
backstrokes the body's currents.
Not a conscious act—

dissolving a reasonable alternative.
In the warm fountain of the showerhead,
he's cupidless, dolphinless. He drifts

between islands of soggy time
unable to secure a shore. He recalls faces
as they slip into the slurry and backwash.

He is fearful facing the sodden map
of the plastic curtain, the latitudes
of shifting steam. He writes his name

backwards on the fogged glass
in case someone with a towel walks
past, recognizing this *aquatica infirma*.

The faucet shut off, the spigot leaks.
Drop by drop, chamber by chamber,
the metal soap dish methodically pings.

He reports, "It was shot by shot.
There's a difference between fighting
and executing. You can hear that."

SPARED NOTHING: AN ALBUM

1   The Invention of Turtles

Between villages, dirt roads, stone walls,
houses confused by their centuries of living
and settling neglect, and the monastery
with its tearing and bleeding icons perched

on a precipice at the edge of the sea. Children
turn two turtles into tanks, as if recalling
the back-handed sketches of Da Vinci.
For cannons they tie sticks to their blunt-beaked

heads. Their scaly legs tread the air,
making no headway in small hands.
Wreathed by branches laid on the ground–
it is the arena of combat where they are forced

to face each other with aimless artillery.
The children shout explosions, spit staccato
gunfire, and tire of these turtles'
wandering disinterest.

A boy strikes a match to the kindling.
Hooped flames crackle waist-high around
two leathery necks stretched beyond prayer.
Never enough for youthful Inquisitions,

another boy empties into the conflagration
a cigarette package stuffed with shiny brass cartridges
from the beginnings of another war.
The children run screaming and diving for cover.

The first bullet fires into the fire.
In quick succession, the whine and ricochet,
spreads flames over the arid slope
of this coastal hill. The children, amazed

at hearing only the hiss of receding waves,
stand and brush off their knees.

2   Already Left

No one is touching the sidewalk
including the man across the avenue.
Heels, toes, soles, are banking
off the air and scrambling higher.

If a shoe does touch the glass-strewn
concrete, it is only to quickly ask
forgiveness before bounding back
and sailing through the cold air

and out of this life. Up one street,
down another, most of the shops
are closed. Across the treeless park,
a boy says, "I like the stumps . . . .

It's like something inside me."
There's no waiting for that final moment
though it's half-expected, half-desired.
It's the only way to escape this city

and never take another boot-bound step.
Everyone: the man in the polished leather
jacket, his back pearled with sunlight;
a mother, her purse bouncing from

her hip into its own orbit as she leaps
over the fallen lamppost; a teenager
with a gym bag slung over one shoulder,
a shopping bag cradled in her arm,

all surprised by their new found lightness;
as they run along a nineteenth-century
cobbled street, suspended over
twentieth-century shadows.

3   Stretcher

Odd for a car driving so fast
that the back hatch door is not
closed. In fact it is wide open,
as the flap of an envelope might

become unglued and its letter
threaten to fall into the surrounding
rubble to be read by ghostly winds.
It's really a common

white wooden door, perhaps
belonging to any one of their houses,
but now projects out the back
of this too-short car. A father

is squeezed in beside it, lying on
his side, hair whipping about his face.
He leans on the smooth wood
with one elbow, and frantically

knocks as the car careens around
an ancient debris-strewn corner.
His son under a blanket beside him
refuses to open the door.

4   The Reporting

They dive behind notebooks
and headstones. They hug
the grass and plant their pens
and pencils in the raw,

newly turned earth. A black
film canister falls from
a vest and rolls
down the gravel path,

exposing its images. Pages
are blown open. A film crew
behind trees on the knoll keeps
recording—one reporter has both

his arms wrapped around her legs,
another has his hands under her arms
as they stumble along under her dying
weight. A young woman holds her mother's

hands as they turn red in black
and white. An old man defiantly
stares off in confused directions.
The procession lies

down among the graves. Her
grandson still waits for the first words
to be shoveled over this sunny
afternoon. It will be written in

the evening news, in the days
to come, in the weary years ahead
that they kill the dead once
and the living twice.

5   Birds of Warmth

No longer mown grass,
no longer flat and chalked
with lime to mark the goals,
to declare the limits of play.

In the middle of the many rows,
the middle of raw and ordered
mounds, a middling man half-bent,
half-kneeling in thin snow,

wearing a sock hat and jeans,
glances up at the looming
hills and the tops of gutted
buildings. He holds an axe

in one hand, swings
at what's left of a tree,
barely boot-high. He will
leave it level with the half-

frozen mud. Across the soccer
field crowded with buried games,
through clouded light, he carries
the splintered wood in his upfolded sweater.

Soon another man appears with
a shovel and the same furtive
glance. He digs up the buried
stump and drags it away.

Later still, a man in a torn jacket
retraces the arthritic paths of roots
and cuts arm-long pieces to feed
a tin stove. The last man sees

that all the city's birds have flown into
the hole and are roosting in the earth.
He carries the hole home to burn.
A fluttering warmth hovers over his face.

6   Spared Nothing

The last emperor of the Austro-Hungarian Empire,
Franz Joseph, lost the war with Italy in 1859,
and the one with Germany in 1866; his brother,
Maximilian, was shot by a firing squad in Mexico

a year later, after he failed to become emperor
of the new world; keeping up with the odds,
his son, Crown Prince Rudolf, killed himself
and his mistress at Mayerling, the family hunting

lodge near Vienna in 1889; and the Empress
Elizabeth, his beloved Sisi, was stabbed to death by
an Italian anarchist in 1898; and when told the news
of his wife, he said, "So I am to be spared nothing."

This mutton-chop, bowler-hatted man continued
to get up at five o'clock from his narrow iron bed
to handle the crumbling affairs of empire.
Franz Joseph lived to see Archduke Ferdinand, heir

to the throne, assassinated in Sarajevo, before he retreated
to his summer house in Bad Ischl and died
in the middle of WWI. But he was wrong; he was
spared the other end of this century, where the splayed

footprints of Gavrilo Princip, the assassin,
are immortalized in concrete on a street corner
among paving stones, as if his legs were still braced
to take aim, where the hunted now run for cover in their

own city, across Princip Bridge and the Miljacka
River, whose banks are lined with shattered
wrought iron lampposts, so each day history
flows darker, even in daylight.

7   Auto-da-fé

On his fifth birthday a boy stops talking
to his father, to three uncles. He stops
talking to his friends, to strangers.
His father and uncles never say another

word to anyone. Wheelchairs block roads,
sidewalks. Empty of arms and legs,
they are not sure which way to turn
to get out of the way.   A man sights down

the length of his crutches, shouts bang.
The shoppers all fall backwards.
The wheelchairs are paralyzed.
Outside town the forest is festive, hung

with shoes and dresses, scarves and blouses,
necklaces that catch the late sun's setting,
and the crudely scrawled messages safety-
pinned to taut ropes. On the street no one

opens a bottle, a can, let's a door slam,
stomps his feet to loosen snow
and mud. Thirst, hunger: common
as weather. The waitress, cotton stuffed

in her ears, refuses to listen to another tale:
the man no one can touch–not his wife,
not his three children; the starving
woman who will only swallow the truth . . . .

The waitress takes the chewed
pencil stuck in her coiffed hair. She points
at the luncheon specials, the ones
starred with catherine wheels.

HOME FRONT

1

One night he was eight,
his mother's lover fired a shotgun
through the closed front door
of the house. His father stood
back braced against the cracked
and weathered wood.

A woman from the house on
the ridge spent frantic minutes
taking doctor's instructions over
the phone before she turned him
over to find a father's lungs
puddled on the linoleum floor.

The next morning the highway
patrol found, in the hollow below
the pond, the shooter beside his gun,
jaw unhinged by his own aim,
the boy's wounded mother
sitting against a sycamore.

2

Three weeks after the Alaskan
Spitz wandered onto the porch
and convinced us he lived here,
a pickup skidded on the gravel,
hit the ditch, and crushed the dog's
pelvis before we'd named him. The boy,

now fourteen, who had watched his father
slide down the door, stared from the passing
school bus, returned from his house
with a rifle, asking to shoot the dog
that was dragging its hind legs
around the yard, wagging its tail.

3

Near the end of December, the two nurses
who lived in the white clapboard house
by the creek, asked about the bullet
that left a clean hole in the living room window,
striking the ornament topping their Christmas
tree, before penetrating the wall.

A month before high school graduation,
a Saturday, the young man, who as a child
held the phone relaying a doctor's useless instructions,
fires endless volleys into the hollow below his house,
hours of random rapid bursts.
Half-a-mile away, cardinals and chickadees

around the yard don't stop announcing
their claims to the air, but I do, wondering
which move: the one to the shed
for the shovel, kneeling to repair
the bicycle tire, weeding dandelions
in the already chaotic garden.

THEBAN TRAFFIC

COLD WET MORNING

"It's called a Spartan shower," Jake shouts. That doesn't stop the complaints pouring from the second floor bathroom.

At first the slapping sounds innocent enough, school of salmon leaping up the cataract of wooden stairs. The house shakes, the medicine cabinet crashes to the sink. Now there's a choice, three pink pills or three shards of mirror to swallow.

The walls are thin enough to swim through. He hears lunging: the shower curtain torn down, the gasping gills of something trying to squeeze down the drain.

A fishy smell drifts along the hall into the kitchen. Jake's lumpy oatmeal is pale as belly-up flounder pounded on the rocks of Tristan de Cunha.

The door flung open, her hair slicked back, Stella stands naked, an immaculate tuna blue, scales of ice clinging to her eyebrows. In a salty soprano, she sings, "We're drowning in two stories of cold."

NEW WAVES ON OLD WATER

Stella travels two thousand miles to sweep up the dust of another relative. Whole mountain ranges pass below her quicker than dreams. She perches on the edge of a continent.

Because they cannot see each other, they cannot exchange diseases though the distant unease is worse. Though they cannot share a bottle of wine their separate glasses overflow with a blush of light. There is a smeared stain in the air like a burning city. Over the phone, he hears her say that's the sun setting over the Pacific.

The trees drop all their leaves. Each leaf falls into its own winter. They heap up words so the fire will thaw whatever has frozen. They throw children in and see how brightly they burn: one in Mexico, one repeatedly breaking his collar bone like a twig of kindling. Another crosses borders, not to flee old wars, but to escape into the skirmishes of marriage.

In a house facing west, Stella sits through the evening. The relentless line of horizon breaks through her. Waves claw the beach, dragging back the half-alive. Slicking the sand, the tide arrives like a rash. Plumes of water crown the tops of rocks. She feels a salty spray blow across her face. Marooned in the forgotten middle of a continent, Jake strolls uneasily looking around at what they've forged of old seas.

MAROONED IN THEBES

It wasn't until he coughed up a mouthful of salt water,
including a wriggling shrimp and a frilly lionfish that had stuck
under his tongue, that he realized he'd washed up on the sea of her
belly. He didn't bother flossing the kelp, picking broken shells from
between his teeth, brushing sand from his sun-scaled lips. Her soft
flesh rose so slowly with her breathing, and he sank so irrevocably,
he didn't realize he was submerged until he gasped for air as the sea
rushed up his nose. He was sucked deep into her navel vortex. He
choked as the descending curve of her belly slid into dark space and
the hull of a great ship disappeared below the horizon. Falling off
the world's maps, he reached the vanishing point. He was marooned
in a salty drop of desire.

HAVING TO ASK

Shipwrecked, he's lying in bed wearing a torn work shirt, the covers pulled back. Jake's knees form two bony pink peaks in a mountain range that doesn't belong on this mattress and continues its synclines and anticlines somewhere else.

The slopes are cleared of trees and heavily terraced. Pencil-thin smoke from village fires scribbles up from deep gorges. Shrouded in clouds, a small herd of wild goats jump across the granite scree. The air in bed is fleshy.

The cat stretched along his left side purrs in his armpit. He's staring at the ceiling, waiting for a flat sky to lift. Last night's moon clings to the small west window.

He feels the ache of paths deeply rutted by oxcarts that lead to barley fields and the torrential rains that run along his thighs. None of this makes any difference.

He doesn't know anyone here. He doesn't know the language. He can't ask for the simplest thing. He lies back, pulls up the covers, and points at his open mouth.

SAILING THEBES

Stella walks upstairs, sits in a stuffed blue chair. She hears a shuffling so distant she can't quite make out what it is or from what direction it's coming. It's the whisper of a twenty-dollar bill taken from a wallet. An old map razored from a book deep in the library stacks. A hand-written note tucked in the pocket of a passing stranger. She tilts her head to the left, to the right. She's not sure what she's hearing. She rises from the chair to get a glass of wine from the kitchen.

A few minutes later, Stella's back and so is the susurrous slippage. She thinks it's the wind tugging on the few winter leaves that haven't fallen from their branches. Out the window everything is still. Not even a half-starved squirrel jumps across the yard. She looks a second time. There's the crinkling of evening's lacquered light stretched to the breaking point, but that's different.

She turns her head straining to hear something more. Stella's glad there's no one in the room with her. This could be the beginning of a diagnosis. To check her hearing, she cups her hand, holds it over her ear. She changes the curve of her fingers, hears a faint roaring, it's the Aegean ebbing in her palms.

NO HELP

Stella's remembering the story that her parents never read to
her, sitting in the small chair beside her bed where she lay, head
sinking into a cloudy pillow, the book glowing in the light from
the Hopalong Cassidy lampshade, pages flashing like the wings of
a plane in moonlight. It's the one about the little Chinese boy who
rides the wind. Actually, he's stolen a worn leather bag that's sealed
tight, sewn closed with wet river reeds that dried in the sun and
made the bag impossible to open, each stitch cinched deep into the
leather. Of course, he doesn't listen to the warning of his elders. He
takes a jade knife, green as spring pasture, and rips the side of the
bag open.

The valley where the boy lived had been perfectly still for centuries,
perhaps an eternity or two. Each leaf in its unmoving place;
dust from the road always falling straight down. Now the trees
are bending to the ground, their leaves spiraling around them
like an aggravated hornet's nest. Peasants' hats sail off to sit on
mountain peaks and become Taoist sages. Sparrows decide it's too
dangerous to fly, drop from the eaves, and hop across gardens. The
thatched village houses lose their roofs. The sky is crowded with
cartwheeling straw. It's a festival. The boy is swept up, riding hard
on the sweating back of wind. Over the horizon his face is in every
cloud.

Today, leaning far back in a chair, she hears the boy moaning.
There's a thin crack in the window frame where he's trying to get in.
After all these years, he's grown tired of being blown here and there.
But only the wind is thin enough to get through. She wraps its long
thin threads onto a wooden spool to keep it from blowing papers off
the desk. After the moans quiet down, she puts the spool into the
sewing drawer. She will sew the boy a shirt of wind.

WHAT STELLA DOESN'T KNOW
ABOUT THE TAILOR

To pin down Ethereal, he runs the tape in and out a couple of times, listening to the snap of inches retreat into its metallic shell. It sounds alert. It sounds in control. It sounds professional.

Scissors rest on the table beside a rolled bolt of black velvet sky. Ready with paper and pencil to disclose the infinite, Jake hasn't forgotten the eraser. He expects to correct vast sums.

He feels his way along the skirt's hem. For more complex calculations, there's plumb bob and radio telescope, if Ethereal would just stand still.

For now, he has a waist measurement and knows her desire for a plunging neckline and low-cut back. Soon everyone in Thebes will recognize the elegant dresser walking the street to Oblivion's house, wearing a boutonniere laced with forget-me-nots.

AMPUTEE

Jake has more jobs than fingers and at least one job he'd like
to cut off. He dreams to be left alone in the garage enhancing the
perpetual motion machine that he's become, racing from counseling
to jogging to philosophy lecture, simultaneously answering phone
calls and letters as he sits at his desk in a windowless room ripe with
old car grease. But really, today's job requires little preparation. He
knows it's always and only a matter of time. He makes plans, the rent
past due, the chasm of debt always gaping wider, it's just one
more paycheck.

The day a flawless blue, a soul staring up too long is convinced,
becomes dizzy, and tumbles into the sky. A shivering wake, the dry
leaves shouldering the road as the procession of sober-colored cars
pass, passing plastic flowers, wilted flags, three dogs by the stone gate,
the child in a far yard bouncing a ball. All become still, so still they
slow the lead limousine until it stops, separating space from time. On
cloudy days, souls walk off into a mist that leaves the suited grievers
in their own moist little bowls, surrounded by polished granite
tablets. The crowning oaks reach out to pull them in the direction
they need to go. On windy afternoons, the mourners are anchored
by their downturned heads, their billowing coats the rotting sails of
beached schooners.

It's so easy, how each moment, in the loosening of time, of space, turns
sacred, falls effortlessly into place, dust to dust, down to the backhoe
that's out of sight. But Jake has so many jobs, so many commitments,
he's a particle in a linear accelerator. There are days he's close to
colliding with himself, close to splitting into something smaller before
mushrooming out of control. He needs a vacation. Not a Caribbean
cruise, not a phoneless motel room outside the city with infinite
cable channels, not a trip to Texarkana. He's got to get away from
the job that he hates most. On blue, wind-struck days, in cemeteries,
Jake vacations with death, standing under miles of sky delivering
apocryphal tales over Thebans he's never known.

BLUE MIGRATION

Jake's in some kind of too late mid-life crisis, not that he thinks in those terms, though he's consumed by a feeling of unease, really a subtle and growing disease, whose diagnosis is not obvious to any of his friends, or health care workers, two types he's strenuously avoided these last months. It could quickly turn deadly, not that there was really any hopeful prognosis, and too easily, cynically, summed up behind his back by "sooner or later."

He turns into the satellite bank's parking lot, the afternoon a perfection of blue—there's nothing to see with his head tilted back into a falling-up sky. On days like this, emergency rooms are crowded with a rush of vertigo cases: sand grains blown off the beaches of patients' inner ears, all who want to leave the planet, be transported, seduced into the infinite, eternal, ethereal, out-of-body, out-of-mind, out-of-this-stinking-place, head-for-the-hills, head-for-the-stars, take-the-money-and-run… wait he's stopped, the only dented, wheel-well rusted, right rear-taillight-missing, no hub caps, car in the lot, that looks half like an abandoned osprey nest. When he opens the door, he's taking flight, moving out onto a limb of sidewalk, and he almost raises his arms to begin flapping.

Jake enters through the double-tinted glass doors, hands in his pockets, there to check his balance, walk the tightrope of accounting, slip past the noose of overdrafts, make a small deposit. The silent TV mounted in one ceiling corner displays the enclosed captions of CNN, morning's stale coffee sits in a silver urn beside the stacked peak of Styrofoam cups. A bowl of Jolly Rogers by the only open teller's window, and in her practiced, mellifluous voice she says, "How can I help you?" and he can't remember, he's a fledgling falling from a nest, a jettisoned rocket booster tumbling through space, an aging man in a too quickly aging moment.

She asks again, and rather than opening his wallet and signing the check, he says in a meek monotone, "Give me all your money," and pulling off his sweat-stained baseball cap to use as a pathetic receptacle, the teller dutifully, awkwardly stuffs the hat and hands it back. He flies out as slowly as he walked in. He's sitting in the car, staring up through the dirty windshield at a single stringy cloud that's cracked the sky, when three police cars careen past, lights flashing. They run into the bank, guns drawn.

Having completed their reports, dusted for fingerprints, reviewed the video cameras, they have no leads. Jake's still nesting in his car when the police leave the bank. It's not clear to him, the money spilled across the passenger seat, wrapped in small bundles like green dominoes, if he's dead or just the soul of a bird in flight.

HOW TABLES LEARN TO TALK

Jake can tell you what and maybe why he pulled back the covers and got up, sitting for a moment on the edge of the bed, taking one conscious breath then another, inflating the body back to life, left hand feeling for glasses on the night stand, chin on chest keeping his head from falling to the floor.

It was around 2 a.m. when the table startled itself awake, realizing it was no longer in the kitchen and hadn't been for hours. With wooden legs and a lumbering Frankenstein gait, it must have sleepwalked into the living room. Paralyzed with fear, it couldn't make it back to surround itself with chairs and so became a ventriloquist, shouting through the woman standing next to it, Stella in a night shirt and naked from the waist down.

It must be moved now, not before breakfast, not after showering, not before leaving for work, but now in the moonlight slipping across the newly waxed floor, dry with shadows. Tables are so hysterical when they wake in the wrong room.

THEBAN TIMING

Hardly a whisper of light at the window. Claws slowly rake the glass. The black cat that sits on the sill has already heard it and wants out, but isn't ready to pounce on the deafly sleeping couple in bed.

The radio alarm begins to rattle loose news: explosions, corruptions, insurrections, floods, houses burglared and burned, the dead mounting every barricade.

Jake threads his way through five cats stretched over the blankets. He's thinking Monday after the last weekend in November and he forgot to reset the clocks to daylight savings time.

Stella wriggles her way through the same crowd of cats, but counts seven overweight purring bodies. Sums unrequited, they both realize they are late or early for work.

Jake hurries upstairs to change the pink digital clock in the study, abandoned by their daughter when she outgrew the color and left for college.

Stella quick to the kitchen to reset the stove clock, and the one that hangs over the kitchen table, a childhood relic, a wooden owl whose eyes stopped counting the seconds long ago and now stare in one exaggerated direction, its heart stuffed with gears.

Downstairs, Stella spins the clock's arms an hour ahead. Upstairs, Jake draws them back an hour. Two hours apart, they've lived in this house for thirty years.

THOSE THINGS

Jake preparing to talk to his son, remembers his father in the hospital bed, slowly entangled and lost amid a maze of tubes, and when from a chair by the window he asked if there was anything his father regretted, he answered, "I'd go to the temple more often and I'd have talked to you about those things."

With long strokes that bent Jake's body like an oarsman, he massaged his father's swollen calves. They'd never touched except to shake hands, and only once did Jake cry to his father's face, when he accused him of not caring, when he was young and still cared, but in those last months, when flowers lined the window sills and Jake read to him, they held hands.

Jake never saw his father naked, and he hasn't seen his son naked in years, though he knows his young body is being driven to collide with others. Yesterday on the basketball court, when his son raised his arms to shoot, he saw dark tangles of hair.

He wonders what more it was his father had wanted to tell him that evening just after he'd learned to drive, when he walked over to the Volkswagen. Jake started the engine as his father leaned toward the window, as if to whisper. Though no one was near, his hand covered the side mirror when he said, "Protect yourself." That was it and Jake backed out of the driveway.

TROUBLE WITH THE EGYPTIAN TRAVEL AGENT

1

The mullahs in their needle-thin towers call prayers out of the
shriveled earth. A hostage, all Jake wants is to forget. The room's
curtains buckle in hot winds. This morning he smells the aromas
of bitter coffee. On the floor below, Oasis Café patrons empty their
thickly brewed cups. He runs his tongue over the crushed blood of
his shattered lips. By noon the heat builds its own ephemeral city,
scooping the heaped odors of the living to the second story. Later
the shadows of windows, of date palms, of dusty white-washed
buildings, are awash in a lacquered light. He can no longer be
certain what city this is. Time and joy have betrayed him. He doesn't
care to see, even if he could raise a swollen eyelid, the window
welded to light and the empty heat-stricken streets. He chokes
on stale sweat mixing with the new efforts of his interrogators to
once again beat their truth into him, the fact of their fists clear, his
identity less so. What is written on the mattress, his clothes, the
floor, are facts he cannot betray. This has gone on so long even the
man who only whispers raises his voice and the other man who has
said nothing begins to crack sore knuckles. Jake grows lighter than
the arguments of his life. Floating near the swan-shaped blades of
the ancient ceiling fan, he is swept out the window, an enlightened
wisp. The interrogators jump to catch hold of his foot, truth quickly
out of reach high above the street.

2

Leaning out the window, enjoying the cool evening breeze, watching it ripple palm fronds, stir the embroidered light and shadows that spread over the town, two men light each other's cigarettes, the smoke trailing from their lips as if a plane or a prophet had crashed somewhere deep in their sun-scarred, eroded faces. Thousands of years have gone into the perfection of their profession, the secret societies of power that covet occult knowledge and unremitting repression. They are relaxed yet know they have failed. A travel agent's mistake when Thebes is not Thebes, still someone has escaped them and lies limp on the floor. They must decide what to do. Should they report this incident to their superior, admit their failure? Should they deny they ever found their victim wandering the bazaar? Is not the truth more important than the petty details that lead from room to room, from town to casbah, from one nameless dune to another, from one life to the other? In one whisper they have loaded the body into a jeep. It is a good night to drive the desert. They know their destination. They have paid their respects to its anonymity many times. In daylight it can be located by the ever-reforming question mark of slow circling birds and at night by the jackal's yawp. They return to town early in the morning, lightened by the dumping of a failed body of truth.

3

Far into the desert, dunes quiver in the after-heat, inviting any man
to lie down with them in a star-stunned night. It's the morning chill
that awakens Jake. The warmth radiating from the sand as the cold
air presses down, confuses his body and obscures the pain. He's still
as the rocks in *Wadi el Hôl*. He rolls his head to one side, eyes puffy
distortions, and sees the desert beginning to discover its shadows.
He can't remember his arrival. His condition, that of a bruised fruit
carried too many caravaned miles, dropped from a saddlebag and
trampled by each passing hour. He's become a memory beyond
remembering. He must find a beginning in this dry place or he will
exist here forever. He recalls being tied into a laundry bag, flung into
the back of an ancient vehicle whose engine hacked and coughed its
way out of town. He was driven hours, dumped at the foot of these
side-slipping dunes. Stones knuckle into his bleeding back. Or is this
the wrong beginning as it must be when Thebes is not his Thebes?
Should he look for a smudge of smoke and the wreckage of a 747?
Surely, this would better explain his ripped lips, his swollen hands,
his purpled chest, and twisted legs. The wind hisses over the sand.
His only companions are fist-sized scorpions crawling near him.
Jake offers his open palms.

4

In the room there is a lateness to each hour. Each minute falls,
as if there is nothing so distant as a minute ago. Walls exchange
austere colors with the passing of day. The ceiling fan a metronome
of uncertainty, tilts toward cruel conclusions as earth wobbles
toward its own seasonal demise. Anymore, he rarely gets up from
his desk to stretch his legs, walk to the window. He knows his
domain is wider than any city or village in this deserted country.
It's subterranean and deeper. Thousands of years are resurrected in
shadows. The obelisks dive into their needled darknesses. Hawk-
headed men walk past his window. Baboons scratch at his door.
An ibis perches on the balcony. Karnak's crumbling colonnade
breaks into immeasurable angles of Luxor. The sun is enthroned
on the Avenue of Sphinxes. He has probed living flesh and found it
wanting. He picks up the glass, leaving a moist ring on the papers
stacked beside the telephone. The melting ice cubes are windows
to that other world he seeks. The sweating glass meets his sweaty
lips and he gulps down sash, sill, and pane. He sees the entire town
with one glance: the narrow streets and squat houses, palms and
minarets, awash in a burning river of light. There's knocking at his
door, slow and dusty as if an ancient temple were collapsing. He
already knows of their failure. He is not a cruel man. He will let
them fail again. He knows the world is truth in the shape of a lie.

5

Days, weeks, Jake no longer can tell the length of his own story.
It did not end as others declared. In town few dared to whisper
of this accidental tourist's absence. Fingers point at the hole on
the street corner where he once stood, in the café where he drank
coffee waiting for his travel agent to return his call. His truth is the
inadvertent lapse in the great scheme between dawn and dusk of
an empire of heat and shadows. When he reaches the well at the
edge of town, where the women gather to fill their buckets, bruises
are no longer visible on his arms, lips are again a continuous line of
scarred words. One eye focuses on the finest details of the present:
the thirteen flies that plague the ass tied to a date tree, the thirteen
lice on the baker's head, the shrill voices of thirteen locusts squaring
thirteen behind the stable. The other eye stares off into a distance
deeper than ruin. There is an unsettling grace in his twisted face.
He has returned with no gifts, no stone tablets, no hope of salvation.
Before he sets out for his other Thebes, it's simple what he says to
anyone who asks: *We suffer the tortured amazement of each day. The
desert must be crossed.*

SAY ANYTHING THEBAN

Lips left on the elevator talking to a beautiful stranger. How much they yearn to return to that last awkward sentence, correct it, smooth out the stutter, say more, but they're gone, fallen into a pocket, caught on a key chain, dangling in a stranger's half-turned door lock.

STELLA CONFESSES TO
THE INVENTION OF THEBES

I heard the fans' spin and hum from the apartment above, the machinery of air mocking me, never wearing out as one bladed revolution followed another, and it was not my own.

Through time's blur, I walk along the Agora past the Blue Note, its doors closed and the rock n' roll inside striking an extravagant repose till dark. I'm one step ahead of the rumor that is always about to catch up and tap me on the shoulder. This time it jumps ahead, crossing rivers, mountains, cities, new-plowed fields, to announce my arrival, but it's been years since I was last in this town, though the way friends talk my shadow is still wet on the sidewalks.

Only I understood that this town, and all the others, invented me as they were my inventions: the bars broken over the backs of blind nights, listening to the clink of ice in the bottom of glasses flushing out another morning, the high facades of Midwestern main streets that led nowhere but the middle west of Thebes, the alleys where I leaned against walls, willing them to stand as those dirt-red bricks willed my standing for another minute, and at last the manicured parks after the ball field lights were turned off, where I lie down into others' green histories.

All written there at my desk, where the tip of a peacock feather, sprouting from a vase, caught a slight breeze, the wake of my arm, as I reached to turn a page. I wasn't startled as the iridescent blues and greens called forth a jungle clearing, a gleaming machete, as the feather fluttered off the desk, and when I leaned forward to search the floor for its perch, it was gone.

In a town of inventions, so are a wife, a husband, a daughter and son, inventions, but the rumors didn't end; one day I nibbled lunch, as if I might turn ascetic, giving up all but an empty bowl and a few shreds of clothing to go begging for a world, but the young girl across the table, puzzled by the waiter's English, said, "There are Chinese people and there are Theban people," and following a thoughtful pause, "The rest are French." I knew that, as any child does before being excused from the table to run outside and press the dull blades of grass against her skin.

The day I walked up to the woman in the grocery, introducing myself out of the blue, that I was "Blue," and said I had dreamed her pushing a child in an otherwise empty shopping cart, her empty purse hanging from her shoulder, the basket's chipped chrome radiant, their faces glowing. I knew someday I would invent a child, memory, tinkering and invention. I knew it was invention that left room for the living, if that is what it could be called as I added my name at the bottom of her crumpled shopping list.

In the book I once signed, a letter has disappeared from my name, leaving the rest of the signature fading, though the funny little picture I drew of a square two-story house on the single parabolic-pen-stroke of a hill, above the two squiggly lines of a river, cling to the page like the house clings to the smoke rising out of its chimney, which is blowing nowhere as it spreads over my name.

Today, over the paper plates heaped with potato salad and roast beef, ice cubes melting in Styrofoam cups, the sports banquet is steeped in self-congratulations: the best year, the best record, the best players, all that I would politely applaud, but even here over the waves of clapping and standing ovations, is a whisper of my flight into rumor, the tongue a poor perch for even one peacock feather.

One summer that will always be mine, all I could hear was the deafening scaffolds of crickets building around the house and the buffoon bullfrogs belching out the night. All I could see from the porch was one or two stars between the heavy canopy of leaves. A humid breeze blew through the branches, almost the pall of dark green chimney smoke, and that was enough, all I ever needed to drift away.

To see the sky smoked by the Milky Way, was to see the lewd, pale-glittering scar of hope, a feather that I swore each of us grasped, however loosely, that left me fluttering over ditches by back roads, where the wrong-turn, the dead end, was what I expected. To be greeted by the ebony howls of dogs beside patched together houses was just another step toward the room that is always found wanting, my imperfections necessary and sufficient for the life of invention, and this invention of leaving.

THE FEAST

BELLY OF THE BEAST

To be properly expressed a thing must proceed from within, moved by its form.
—Meister Eckhart

Every man takes the limits of his field of vision for the limits of the world.
—Arthur Schopenhauer

BEFORE THE BEGINNING

This is what happens when he stands face to face with no, and no the true genius of the world. No, he won't sit on the potty, and so he sits wrapped in his mess for the rest of the day. No, he won't struggle with putting on his galoshes on a rainy morning, and so he walks to school barefoot, all the other kids laughing. No, he won't stand on the chair, lean among the flowers to kiss the face of someone who once loved to playfully cheat him at cards and torment him in other small delicious ways, then his frightened face is shoved up against death. No, he won't give the older boys his jacket, and after school is chased all the way home, barely staying ahead of the heavy swinging belt buckles. No, he won't eat his broccoli or spinach, or anything green that looks like the squashed insides of a caterpillar, and he falls asleep at the table, then falls out of the chair. No, he cannot say no, but he does. No, he won't go to the barbarous city of Nineveh, but instead heads for Tarshish, across a storm-riddled sea where he draws the short lot and is thrown overboard for God-only-knows-what-reason, and ends up living inside a great fish. Yes, no is the genius of the world.

NO-JON-AH
from "Belly of the Beast"

No one notices even on days when he stands in the cashier's line at Wal-Mart, holding a water-filled plastic bag with bright swimming things that he is a man who lives inside a fish. Actually, he lives in a house he carved out of the inside of a living fish. He can't remember how long he has sat at the one table built from a giant fish scale. He rarely opens his eyes anymore, not because there isn't any light, a fish oil lamp flickers in the middle of the horny-scaled table, but because he feels better not watching what passes below the invisible floor of his rib-roofed house. His eyelids slammed shut when he thought he heard cries for help pass below him. The guttering flame from his burning blubber, scraped from the walls of his fishy house and poured into the seashell lamp, only cast gurgling shadows. He can see nothing but the viscous percolation, the amorphous dissolving of sea into fish.

He is left with only the faint echo of something, the insidious scratching and scrapping of hermit crabs making homes inside his ears. He can't say if what he thinks he heard was yesterday, last week, or years ago. But if it was yesterday, the pain is still sharp enough for him to long for a dust-choked earth. If it was last week, the grief is already being carried away in a stream of memories. If it was years ago, then the tide has continued to rise and he's now awash in a cataclysmic flood, on his last gasp, treading water. He's planning to build a submarine to save all the creatures floundering at this depth. He knows that it is only those of us who can't swim who will save ourselves.

JONAHIC DISLOCATIONS
from "Belly of the Beast"

When the great fish finally slurped up every corner of the ocean down to the last drops hidden in the crevices of the Great Barrier Reef, down to the pools bottomed in the Java Trench, draining the vast abyssal hills, turning the Yangste and Yukon alluvial fans into cracked mudflats, baring the submerged roots of the Lesser Antilles to the Bahamas and forming a range of mountains with tropical summits, when at last the fish sprawled at the mouth of the Amazon as the last whisper of the longest current slipped between its lips, it lay sprawled, bug-eyed, gasping, its body bloated and misshapen by the world's oceans and seas; and Jonah in his fishhouse was exhausted from frantically plugging the leaks, mopping his invisible floor, a one-man bucket brigade, as the Atlantic and Pacific rushed past, the Black Sea and the Baltic, the Mediterranean and Lake Superior. He was pruned, his skin shriveled, fold after translucent fold submerging into itself. He felt salted and pickled. The great fish lay unmoving except for its archaic gills slowly fanning up a dust storm that engulfed Brazil. It looked as if it swam to the end of the earth.

Jonah wading waist deep through his rib-roofed house, trying to keep his table and lamp from floating into a sopping oblivion, was ready to throw in the towel, when the fish arched its continent-long back, slapped down its tectonic plate of a tail and lunged forward, coughing up all that it had swallowed, making rivers run backward, popping the polar ice caps like just-opened soda bottles, setting the Titanic down on Broadway in New York City, leaving Jonah beached on the boardwalk in Bombay. Jonah turned to face the gaping mouth of the great fish. It slithered backward into the sea and belched. From its fishy breath he heard the rasping of the thousand-thousand holy names and he dived back into the dark maw.

FISH@NET.COM
from "Belly of the Beast"

There must have been a great battle, or else his great fish was on fire. Perhaps it had been torpedoed and was soon to sink. Smoke billowed from the maw of its throat. His ribbed cavern blackened. He thought he could hear the blare of trumpets, the irregular thunder of explosions, the gnash and scrape of immense machines grinding together. His rib-roofed house began to choke from acrid odors of burning diesel and flesh. He lay down on his invisible floor, hoping not to die in spasms of coughing. He saw sparks sputter, fly through the air, the silhouettes of men running at each other across a stark, cratered landscape, hysterical men shouting and waving bayonets, then falling into each other's arms and then to their knees, then falling even lower, row after row crushed into the raw, mothering dirt. He shook in amazement, quaked in fear, clung to the sides of his beloved fish, but he couldn't take his eyes off the erupting streaks of light tracing the twisting miles of barbed wire like the nerves of a monstrous dying animal. Then the room filled with static. The invisible floor darkened. The battery that he'd salvaged from a crate of floating debris died. The laptop screen glowed a solid gray then blackened. He flipped the switch, the mouse with its wire tail sinking into the sea. He knew for certain, no news is good news. The great fish's stomach rumbled on, devouring history, headed for Omaha Beach and Agincourt.

WHALULAR *THROBOSIS*
from "Belly of the Beast"

He lit his shell lamp and held it outside the window. What was the
slow dull throb that at first he attributed to the onset of a migraine
caused by sitting too long in the blubbery dark? Here in a tower of
spiraling narwhal tusks, he could discover, delineate, pontificate
on the ichthyosaural prime mover. He could contemplate the first-
cause and the final-cause throb, the epistemological throb and the
ontological throb, the pain-in-the-ass throb and the crotch throb, and
still not move an inch.

Standing at the window, he saw the inside of his great fish filling
with the heart of a city in need of angioplasty: all its arteries clotted
with traffic, its gleaming headlighted blood at a near standstill, its
lungs black and exhausted, rivers discolored and syrupy, the park
trees leafless. He swore not to chug another bottle of his home-
brewed fermenting fish.

But it was no delirium tremor. From this height, high in the
belly, where the ribs curved up into the studded-stars, sparkling
with the remnants of the last backwash of cosmic debris, up the
many rickety rungs of ladders, frayed ropes and tow-rope-thick
varicose veins, along greasy precipitous ledges, that all led to his
bone-roofed hermitage, he could see the present claiming a broken-
down past, struggling toward a whimsical, consummate future, and
then the lights began to fade in one section after another of the city,
a massive power blackout, a heart attack, the light clots, and then he
realized he was staring down at the last gulp of phosphorescent red
tide and a night of throbbing indigestion.

KEEPING WHALE HOURS
from "Belly of the Beast"

It really could be. Yes, it really could, and that's what he keeps repeating to himself in admiration of the grand conception. It's the first time in days he has stepped out of his house balanced on its blubbery edge. He descends the kelp and bone ladders. He is whistling the latest pop ditty, heard on the radio before the batteries weakened and the acid bubbled forth, corroding the transistors. Yes, he is on his way, carrying a sheaf of shark fins under his left arm, gripping an air-bladder briefcase, swinging his shell lamp. His shadow leaps forward and back, as if he is in a hurry, bounces up and down, as he swells in importance with each step. He stops in front of each rib and knocks, more than half-expecting it to swing open, his pale knuckles hanging in midair in a gesture of authority. When no one answers, he posts the fin on the calcium-white door and moves on. In fact, for full effect he hangs from each bony arc a deep-sea fish, the one that lights its own way with exaggerated glowing needle-thin teeth and carries its own flesh-waggling neon lure attached to its head. Finished, he sees banks of fin-slapping fluorescent lights stretching down a whale of a hallway. When he reaches the last door that won't ever open and posts the cartilage that will never be read, he realizes that for a moment it was something to do. He turns around and forces himself slowly back up the tiers of swinging ladders and sits down in his rib-roofed house, headquarters for cetacean world tours.

ORPHEUS FISHLOVE
from "Belly of the Beast"

For hours he could hear someone wandering far below, kicking
at the debris of civilizations: elegant, cracked clay urns, twisted
steamship paddle wheels, eye-white bleach bottles, clouded miles
of tangled fish nets, tumbled Ionic columns, heavy stone calendars
stained with sacrifices, arm- and legless marble statues, chariots,
tireless Edsels, windowless Studebakers—the overwrought fever of
centuries and the overwrought digestion of a fish's galactic hunger.

It was a man, he was certain of that, the heavy clank and clang,
the scrape and rasp, moving immovable objects, searching for
something, shoving aside granite griffins and defaced sphinxes, the
entire edifice of religions and astrological projections, Hammarabi's
Code and the Magna Carta. But it was the words, the first he had
heard in years, maybe minutes, he didn't know, time lost and
forgotten in this cavernous gut, and the phrases so ethereal, he
began to swoon. He cowered below his window sill, shaking his
head in disbelief, now that the hallways of his ears were suddenly
drained, soaked corridors dry, his head threatening to explode with
the melodies that entered and would not leave. The stranger never
stopped singing of what he'd lost, the endless search, the repeated
failure. Every inch of his pale, flaccid skin ached to be wrapped
in the thigh's curve, the arm's heated embrace, the hand's delicate
probing and firm stroke.

Listening from his high-house perch, he heard songs blending
the murmur of the sea and the murmur of the dead, and he grew
afraid. He could see the flicker of the torch that the man held high
and the lyre he carried in his other hand. His back was turned as
he walked farther away, past pyramids and earthen mounds. The
stranger was searching for something else, for an uncivilized love,
one with the power to tame three-headed dogs, boil away rivers of
forgetfulness, stand an army of spirits at attention against the will of
wind. He wanted to tell the stranger he hadn't gone far enough; he
needed to go deeper than this junkyard, beyond where even great
fish swim, but his voice had drifted off in a corked bottle. When the

torch flicked its last spark and the man was out of sight, continuing his journey toward an immense, if not infinite loss, he sat safely behind his dripping blubber walls and again swore devotion to his mute fish, and wept.

SUN SCREEN
from "Belly of the Beast"

He desperately shields his eyes from the sun. The shade of four fingers isn't enough. Too new out of the flickering dark, he can't see a thing. Placing his palms over his eyes, he stares at X-rays, the surf-jumbled bones of his hands clearly visible to him, delicate as the wings of flying fish, but hardly looking strong enough to hold up the net of his sagging skin. Not to be dragged back by the undertow, he claws at the waves. The gentle rocking of each swell threatens to topple him, as he half-walks, half-scuttles toward the shore.

The light splintering on the green surface spears every exposed inch of his skin. He's an exotic specimen waiting to be collected. He staggers under the glaring blue magnitudes of sky. He passed through hours of the sea's churning labor, the great fish's slow dilation, and the final moment when its throat clamped down and then spewed him forth—his ladders and house finally reaching beyond mere irritant.

His translucent soles shoot the searing heat of the sand up into his knees. He's dazzled by the bright shards of colored towels spread over the beach. He quickly stumbles into the shade of an umbrella, where a woman lies, every inch of her exposed, every inch tan. He sits down confused, ready to speak the prophecy of her doom, asking if this is Ninevah, but feeling the primal throb.

Speechless, she stares at this thing that's come from the sea and belongs back under the waves. It's a talking page ripped from an anatomy book: blue veins pulsing under his skin, the shadows of bones rising from the fleshy depths of arms and legs, lips unable to hide the bald grin of teeth. Startled, she answers no, this is North Miami Beach. She introduces herself, Jessabelle, says she sells Mary Kay Cosmetics, and knows just the product for his condition. If he agrees to let her use before-and-after photographs for a sales promotion, it would be a no-charge consultation. The sea casting up its pastels, the scattered clouds powder puffs, a blush of sky marking the sun, they leave the beach in her pink Cadillac.

PSALM 66
from "Belly of the Beast"

He didn't have to swim a thousand miles—he drove, and now he
simply pushes open the building's double doors, steps out onto
the cinder-ridden sidewalk, and inhales the decomposing odors of
flotsam and jetsam. At this rise in elevation, lined with century
oaks, punctuated with an intersection where cars feign stops before
speeding on, all the sea would run downhill, unless the hill itself is
a slow welling up of sea.

Before crossing the street, he searches for the flash of scales, a fin
flip, the turbulence of a school of tuna roiling the sunstruck surface.
The morning-wet whale-back asphalt glistens. Standing on the curb
he has nothing to say. He has listened to the doomsayers and the
prodigal sons, the assessors and the hedonists, the elected and the
lost, and he casts his lot into the depths, crosses through a storm
of traffic, and is coughed up into another day of work, a fishy odor
lingering on his clothes. A small driftwood picture frame, sitting
near a corner of his desk, floats these watery words:

> From the ends of the oceans will I cry unto thee,
> when my heart is overwhelmed:
> lead me to the fish that is higher than I.

NINE LIVES ON THE WESTERN FRONT

At the table in a voice that no longer belongs to her but to this century: echoing down twenty-feet-high sound barriers along the shoulders of freeways; from person to person in unemployment lines, who expect nothing more than the line to be there tomorrow; on street corners where rumors flex their muscles at passing girls and they still fall for it; and in this kitchen steeped with yellow light, she announces the unequivocal success of their failures.

Too quickly, their lives are beyond them and not theirs, herded across borders, walked out into the middle of fields and left there, shoved through doors into unspeakable rooms. Now across from her sits a man, a mere vehicle, her husband, Jonah, whose mother half a century ago became pregnant and married the conquering army of a war-ravaged continent. According to his wife, he was simply a means to an end, and now she's left with this broken tool to wrench the world back into place. She lifts Jonah's hands, curls his fingers around two empty beer bottles, and points outside. Then she points to herself; long before amniocentesis, there was the avalanche of her parents' disappointment, wanting a boy, only a boy, then having to face decades of her. The avalanche sweeps across the table to their son sitting between them. He continues to eat, face down to his plate, as if nothing is being said. She demands to know what he thinks he's doing—trying to be like his parents?

The husband, speechless, recalls a childhood game he played called hot potato. He sat in a sandbox with friends, one in each corner, throwing something back and forth, a plastic bucket or ball, but instead of a scalding potato, they imagined a hand grenade. He can't remember how they decided that it exploded and one of them would leap backwards out of the sandbox, arms and legs thrown outward, a human asterisk, or if the shrapnel-shredded flesh was ever more real than a scraped elbow or knee, and exactly how many times they could die before dinner.

SLEEP OF ANGELS

Jonah gives the bed wings and arranges them like the blades of
a helicopter. Many smaller beds fly through the room. They are
plentiful as whining mosquitoes, their wings creating a celestial
annoyance. Whoever enters the room is driven mad by visions
of perfection, and in order to survive, invents lesser beds, ones
with only two wings. These beds take off and land like bombers
returning from missions over World War II Europe—Berlin and
Dresden. Whole squadrons, trailing sheets of smoke, approach
the room's running lights. They crash land into the night stand,
knocking off the clock and the flight crew's portrait that is always
missing one person. They slam into walls already discolored from
the leaking engines of an ancient sleep. Some land with only one
wheel strut down and spin off the edge of the bed. Some skid on
their bellies the length of the mattress before bursting into flames.
Another is landed by the tailgunner, the rest of the crew wounded
and dying. One bomber lands with no crew at all. This last plane
shows no sign of damage, not a single bullet hole. No blood smeared
across the control panels or splattered on the windshield. The crew
has vanished. This plane sits at the base of the headboard for weeks,
everyone afraid to touch it. Finally, it's swept under the bed and
never spoken of again.

The dead are so much easier to care for, lined up and counted,
smiling under their sheets, still wearing their leather jackets and
helmets, recalling how peaceful it was in their oxygen masks,
flying above the ceiling and staring down at the rolling clouds. For
those crews that must ditch in the sea, the pillow cases open into
parachutes, dumping all the tousled heads hidden in their linens.
As for the rest that exploded with their targets—factories filled with
mothers and fathers—they have already begun free falling, and
because guards become prisoners, and prisoners turn into guards,
no prisoners are taken. Back in bed, another mission completed, the
debriefing over, the damage assessed, the pilots lie back and sleep
the sleep of angels.

BEING ITS TIME

In a small Baltic town, on a cold overcast day that could have been yesterday a century ago, and for all practical possibilities will probably be tomorrow a century from now, and whose indeterminancy turned the maypole in the hay-stacked field just east of the last half-timbered houses into a spear stuck in the frozen ground by a falling warrior of Valhalla—here Heidegger slipped beyond his and anyone else's journal. He abandoned future biographers who might scour the town for street corners where the great thinker stood, so they could ponder what he might have pondered, such as seeing his reflection in the window of the shoe-repair shop. He stepped away from the preponderance of philosophers who would keep turning the pages until they were blank as the coming Arctic snow. It was there at the small desk in the inadequately heated third-floor room, which was really an attic he rented under an alias, where each breath hinted of the last, that he first wrote that *the only thing worth thinking is the unthinkable.*

Heidegger had dipped his stork-white quill into the inkwell and flown into the dark, not knowing if he would ever return. There was elation among those who thought he had given birth to the unknown or, less, that he made the improbable probable. Accident became coincidence, coincidence synchronicity, and synchronicity the fine tuning of the cosmos. Whole tired towns swore off potatoes and turnips, and starved, believing they could live on the light of his thinking. These emaciated towns became known as the first voluntary pogroms. A man bloodied his face trying to run through a wall, but the rumor persisted of his success. Throughout the country large bandages flowered over noses, as if an early sign of spring. Women hanged themselves from ceilings, hoping to get closer to heaven, and had to be cut down. Finely braided rope burns around delicate necks became high fashion. Photographers began keeping records of the soul using glass negatives. To be crowned unthinkable became the rage.

For others the century was a curse. There was the unthinkable factory job, the unthinkable war that led to the next unthinkable war, and the unthinkably cold tenements in the cities. The unthinkable kept looming larger, leading to the unthinkable bomb. And then there's the unthinkable God enslaved to eternity, and Heidegger's own unthinkable being thinking in a darkening world.

DELPHIC CHICKEN

"Crito, I owe a cock to Asclepius; will you remember to pay the debt?"
—Socrates after his hemlock

What about Socrates' chicken? After he left the sobbing cell, Crito found Asclepius in a local brew-pub, stumbling through waves of fermented barley. Crito, disgusted with such a public display of grief, not realizing that with each drained tankard Asclepius was being washed farther up on the shore of knowing himself as a pounding headache, walked out and left the debt unpaid. Did Crito then set Socrates' chicken free, leaving Socrates to be known as a legendary bad credit risk; leaving the rest of us with the debt that can never be paid, *gnothi seauton*?

And what kind of life did a destitute chicken live, having lost its master, who was also its slave, feeding and watering it every day, eyeing its plumpness, feeling its firmness, waiting for that ravenous philosophical hunger that wrings hands and necks? There is no getting up from the chopping block. Could it have wandered the alleys of Athens, followed by reverent whispers, "There goes Socrates' chicken"; followed by those people down on their luck, who had made ill-considered investments in goats or been cuckolded for the dozenth time? Did they approach the clucking myth, believing the wisdom of a chicken could stop the widening cracks in their Humpty-Dumpty lives?

Holding out their hands, they delved the gallusic signs: If the chicken pecked too hard and drew blood, that meant no, unless the trickle flooded the lifelines across their palms, which meant the tragedy of their lives would reach historic proportions, and a footnote would be reserved for them, thereby transforming the near- to farsighted and far- to nearsighted in their quest to join the immortal gods; or even better, if the chicken ate the bloodied grain from their open hands, then yes, they should try again to salvage their marriage or underwrite another ship of oil-filled amphoras from Ephesus. In Delphi the capitals at the tops of marble columns are scrolled chicken feathers.

LOST CREW
Book 6
. . . the victim and the executioner.
—Baudelaire

The snow begins to melt, and the yellowed grass spikes up from a poorly seeded lawn left half-finished by a construction crew. He sits in a parked car thinking it looks more like clumps of hair left after chemotherapy or radiation, or whatever it is we choose to do to ourselves after we discover that it's too late, that it's been done to us.

This isn't to blame the victim, we all are victims, and not to diminish the executioners either. They hone blades on their own histories, which is also us. From that first eye-opening moment when our luminous gray irises float on small fat faces, when we see through it all and never see a thing again, when we are nothings with limitations, it's really the world falling in on us.

The random patterns turn our small hairless heads, if we have the strength, and no matter which way we look there is something falling into our nothingness. If we cry, the liquid lenses just magnify and bring whatever it is closer and upside down in the sliding of our salts. We can't stop the faces from falling down on us: mother, father, siblings, all the strangers that we later search for, flipping through photo albums, phone books, skimming rush hour crowds on city streets, for the rest of our and their lives, believing there's a chance we can resolve, perhaps understand that one haunting glimpse from so long ago.

In jaundiced lighting of airport terminals, slouching in stiff chairs, we exhaust ourselves half-recognizing each traveler who passes, the concourse filling with half-recollections, thinking this is how they might look twenty, thirty years later, leading a child or carrying a briefcase, walking arm-in-arm with someone we should know, smiling, waving goodbye, hello. We must restrain ourselves from running up to them, saying, "Aren't you...? Did you know...? Do you live in...? Did you go to school at...?" Restrain ourselves if only to save our reputations and conceal the desperation, knowing we carry this same burden around with us, that we are only half recognizable to anyone else, half of what someone's searching for,

yet we will wear out our knees trying to make up the difference
with the half of us that hasn't drifted beyond our reach, the half that
someone else is sure they know, though we have never met them before.

He sits in a parked car staring at the snow's conflagration,
the glare off the remaining sooty patches, and flips through the
pages of Homer that he has promised himself to read. He catches
a movement out the corner of his eye, and wonders if it's someone
who thinks he knows him. Quickly he turns his head, glances in the
rearview mirror, but there's only the smoldering shadow of Troy.

HISTORICA DENTATA

It started when Jonah's teeth no longer fit comfortably in his mouth. It was not that they were growing like dandelions on a golf green, or that he had fangs hanging over his lips and down the sides of his jaw, as if he were headed toward extinction with the saber-toothed tiger. One day his teeth were rooted in sand. In the mirror their yellowed enamel reminded him of picket fences around summer beach houses—a gummy placid sea visible between each board obliquely bent under the weight of sailored skies. His mother washed his mouth out with sand. His breath turned salty and smelled of sea wrack: twisted kelp and chipped brachiopods, translucent vertebrae and oil-soaked cormorants, spiny urchins and flaccid squid. His friends thought he was a sea of babbling, that he was backstroking through a riptide of gibberish when asked the simplest question. It was just his tongue trapped and drowning in his mouth's tide pool.

Another day Jonah's teeth are poker chips tossed on the green felt of his gums. All around the table, faces are tense. The edges of brows suffer minor tremors. The bets are in: past lives, a month of Sundays, once in a blue moon, the future tense. The croupier looks into the eyes of the players; they float in a bottomless waiting, the last card about to be turned. When his mouth is shut, his teeth are a sealed deck. The dealer peels back his lips, makes the first cut and shuffles, there's no sense of order left: canines shoving out incisors, molars replacing front teeth, bicuspids ready to fall down his throat. When his finned tongue lunges in and out between his lips, they play "go fish." It's all very confusing to him, sitting on a stool with a mouthful of seawater, little enamel boats moored to his gums clinking together. Holding only a pair of deuces, the sails of his teeth burn and sink toward Valhalla.

But when his teeth began to trumpet, graze from one side of his mouth to the other, and his head shifts under their ponderous weight, Jonah stops standing straight, falls toward one precipice or another, and with a lumbering vertigo sway he walks down the hall. He makes an appointment with a dentist. Hanging on the antiseptic glare, suspended in the elevator music gurgling from the ceiling, the dentist smiles and says, "It's your age. Your teeth are beginning to drift." He thinks of Hannibal, forever the showman, how he ordered burning torches tied to the horns of a thousand oxen before stampeding them toward the Roman soldiers trapped in the dark; enough to rattle any pagan's teeth. Even elephants couldn't save him. Publius Scipio pulled all Hannibal's teeth at Zama in Numidia, and sent them as trophies to Rome. Hannibal always wore a ring with a secret chamber for such occasions. He would sail off in a dental chair before being captured alive.

SEA OF TIME

It's a simple loss. Monday morning he woke, thought it was Saturday, and lay there in the warmth of his own depression, blankets pulled up to his chin. He stared at the arms of the clock that kept lifting an unfathomable weight, until he heard the empty echo of the shower and knew he had to get ready for work.

This past evening, he lay down on the couch, the music from the radio rising and falling, a gentle undertow, enough to pull him under. A single small lamp casts a circle of light onto the worn-out waves of the rug. This is all it takes for him to wake to Friday and not Tuesday. It's not only sleep that misplaces days for him, in the middle of a conversation he asks the date. Told it's Wednesday, his face is all loss, a shell-shocked blankness, as if he turned his back to the street and found himself wandering the ravaged fields of Verdun nearly a century ago. He knows his honor lies in the elegance of his defeat.

He finds defeat early this morning, driving to work, when he glances along the street and sees a woman hunched over in a wheelchair, a small dog sitting in her lap. He is doubled by the mirror of doubt. Should he stop, ask if she is all right? Afraid of what he will hear, he drives on, only to circle the block to see if she is still there. She is, hasn't moved, and he pulls over to the curb. He asks and can't understand the reply from the down-turned face. Now he's committed to unraveling the slurred speech. It's the battery-operated wheelchair that has run down. He doesn't know how long she has sat there folded into her chair on a day of below normal temperatures with her dog in her lap. He tells her he's leaving to call the police. After he places the receiver down, he feels this happened on a different day, and he returns to the street to find the woman in the wheelchair gone.

On his birthday, when he was thirty-one, he wasn't thirty-one, he was thirty-two, but he didn't know that at the time. It didn't make sense to him for three days. In fact, he continues to search for the missing year. Its loss is a phantom limb, an itch just beyond his reach. It is hair that continues to grow around his heart, grass gone to seed on his tongue—the hulls of empty hours and days bleached pale in a ghost year. Yet he is here and there, the pulse uninterrupted in his wrist. How could this happen? He was convinced that his friends, his wife, were simply wrong. He pulled his driver's license from his wallet. He searched for his birth certificate. He sat with pencil and paper and recalculated. He counted on his fingers as time grew more incomprehensible, a phantom amputation.

In the Candle Light Lodge the smell of disinfectant hangs in the air day and night to preserve the aged. The old man sits in a chair by the window in the light of a winter day. He doesn't move for hours. He waits in the timeless tiled corridors marred only by the call for lunch and dinner. On the wall are pastel prints of paintings with rivers and parks, the same people always picnicking on a blanket, the anemic light, the colors smeared across their faces. With a heavy Polish accent he says, "I'm too old, but I'm no different from a boy in here," and he touches his head, "but I can't even jump over the fence in the yard to save the bird from the cat. I survived a labor camp and Dresden but not this time. "

One day in New Guinea, a young Cassowary, carrying shield and spear through the jungle, walks leisurely with a visitor from far away, one who has the power to fly. The nervous visitor suggests that they hurry or they won't arrive at the village before night fall. The naked man stops, turns to say, if they walk faster the sun will set more quickly, if they take their time, the sun will match their steps.

One morning he looks in the mirror, waiting for his eyes to focus, and sees the deepening shadows. He knows he will never hear the stalled traffic, the arguments, the parties, or lie down against the soft belly of that year, its light already old and bending beyond his life.

FIELDS OF THENAR

BEIRUT

Machine guns inhabit the rooftops
like hungry crows.
Bullets peck the library
city hall the cobble streets
Allah's forehead.

To the east
mountains belch dust
as artillery fires into the city
planting the bloom of brown orchids
on the beach apartments
on the Hilton
in courtyards filled
with the shattered rosary of bricks.

People are opening their bodies
for the world to read
the print still wet and so red
it pours out a stoplight
on Broadway and Ninth
in downtown Columbia, Missouri.

AMERICAN HISTORY

When you have traveled this far
the steel doesn't join in the distance.
One rail loses sight of the other.
Oaks no longer grow
to tie their direction together.

No train swells then disappears.
Its heavy iron just hangs there
shaking the earth
(as it did one night
 along the Mississippi
 as I slept in high grass
 near the tracks)
until the moon cracks
and the water gives its last breath
to a belly-up channel cat.

Fifty years from now
I will still pick
that metal fist out of my jaw
and listen
to something howl its terror dry
far back in the eroded hills.

SHE CALLS

It's the telephone again.
I must answer and listen closely.
Her voice is distant
blurred in a maze of electricity
as it passes over country
we do not know.
For miles she confuses
the hawks and swallows
that sit on her sentences.

She gives no explanations
no words of assurance.
She revives no memories.
Her body is a legend
raging in the red clay fields
of an Oklahoma evening.

She wants the words to hurt.
She beats the receiver
against the ground
trying to shake a voice loose.
I say nothing.
She must invent her losses.

SEPTEMBER

bright light molting
seed falls into seed.

the long sentence of black birds
(dark stem of air
winged root
wild rumor of corn
of snow
scarred light)
leaves the field
and is composed
low over the trees.

maple leaves cover the garden
edges curled
brittle palms open.
these birds pour down.
they search
the withered tomatoes
split squash, rotting melons
for careless messages
of another year.

MARCH

these fields
are mud-covered creeks.
where there was no water
fish now swim.

tonight men engrave ships
on their forearms
launch their bodies
into a drowning sky.

they smile like flooded barns
that touch their feet
on shifting bottoms
then rise in pieces.

behind sand bags
on sagging dikes
there are people
unable to swim.

they build bridges
praise false gods.

MAY

warm tonight
and the black birds listen
to what they have not heard
all winter.

there is the distant glimmer
of city lights
in the cattails—
the moon a thin lamp.

the streets are filled
with insects speeding into life.
in every cell
there is a telephone ringing.

near the pond's dim edge
a toad tongues
the night
with questions.

MYSTERIES
IN THE PUBLIC DOMAIN

HANDMADE TABLE

It's midnight; the lights
are off. Hands glow
in their own concentration

like someone else's gloves,
thin and old, the wrong size,
and out of style.

They shake in the only
world they know.
On a scratched oak table

two hands are folded;
the right cupping the left,
the left tight as a fist.

SHAW'S GARDEN

Today carp crowd
the water under the bridge,
fish of such mixed color
and shadings,
surfacing and submerging
before they can be named.
They swim back and forth,
around in circles,
their mouths opening into
a school of delinquent invitations.

I'm told some boys jumped
the fence one night
to swim past bonsai miniatures,
the raked gravel gardens
that seem to boil
out of the ground.

This first hot summer afternoon
I have no desire to plunge
into this murky man-made lake.
Sunday strollers
crowd the railing
to toss their bread crumbs.
Fish puncture the pond
with a speech too slow
for us to hear.
They struggle over
each other until pushing
the spectacle of fins down
a blue and white streaked carp
is completely out of the water
walking on an earth
of slippery scales.

EVE'S RIB

*The opposite of a correct statement is a false
statement. But the opposite of a profound truth
may well be another profound truth.*
                    —*Niels Bohr*

Adam watched a torrent
of muscle chase a mare
across a field of short grass
as it curled its lips,
nipping her neck,
carrying on as if a horsefly
was tearing at its rump.
It raced back toward
the tree line, leaping
the ravine, then turning,
returning, rearing his
front hooves, coming down
on either side of her back,
the pistons of his flanks
fast firing.

Knowing the handful of dust
he was, Adam wandered down
to the creek. In a rootless,
rockless place he worked
a hole in the earth,
softening it with water,
lining it with mud.
Down and done
he lay back.

When Lilith arrived,
Adam came running,
threw his hands down
on either side of her back,
but she jumped up
off her bruised knees,
and walked out leaving him
far ahead of himself.

At last he fell asleep.
When he woke, she lay there
sleek as a swan
until she opened her eyes
and turned toward the Shadow
blowing away in the grass,
but it was too late
to change anything.
That night, in a field
covered with stars,
Eve's fingers skipped
from rib to rib
not believing a word.

TWO POEMS FOR
THOMAS HART BENTON

1 Persephone

It started so simply
a picnic by the pond
the broad leaves of the grape
like spiral stairs
ascending the oak trunk
where she sits
turned away from the sun
and the mules standing
harnessed to wagon and thresher.

The ripe fields spill
their morning heat.
Steam rises from the wet wheat
and before she could say no
light's warm hand
pulled off her shoes
unbuttoned her dress
and she lay back in the curl
of a bulging tree root.

Her arms folded behind her head
white as the branches of a sycamore
skin smooth
as water-worn stone
the hip's turned hollow
hides everything.

There he waits half-hidden
behind the thick trunk.
He stares through the leaves
face eroded as earth
ready to steal her down
his two mules
patient as winter.

2 Susannah and the Elders

I know you're too naked
that's why you clutch
the broken oak branch
ready to swing at the water
if it touches you
too soon or the wind
with its uninvited hand
that has already memorized
the places you try to forget.

Over your shoulder
beyond the screen of trees
on the far side of a hill
sits a church with its thick
steeple jabbing the sky.
By the scattered headstones
on the west side
of the white clapboard
a pair of mules stand
solemn as monks.

Do you beat the water
for telling you too much
the open and dark story
of your thighs
or is this branch what you throw
at the widening eye of water
where others swim in dreams?

Their desire is you
sitting on the limestone ledge
feet dangling in the creek
and behind the whispering rushes
others abandon their houses.

COUNTRY WALTZ

When will you dance

in a couple of minutes
when you are done shredding cabbage
cooking beans
answering the letter that hasn't arrived

When will you dance

after another cup of coffee
when the bills are paid
after a late lunch
when the cows are back in the barn
from hillside pasture

When you are one death closer

When memory's cold leaf
falls into your hand

When the hay bales are stacked
two high around the outside of the house
and the kitchen windows
are opaque with steam
while winter gnaws at the chimney
unraveling its bone of smoke

When will you dance

after the floor is swept and waxed
and the beat slows to a bruised heart

When you stand by the gate
to say goodbye to another shadow
and bless the night sky.

INTERRUPTION

For a moment
I couldn't remember
what brought us
to this place
flat on our backs
and naked. We should
not have been talking
or trying to talk.

The room was too
still, the house
even more so.

The bed was a small
organ, and in the middle
of a long slow stroke
when the hand
is an exquisite mind
the phone rang
and like a fool
I answered.

A small shaky voice
from the twentieth century
crawled into my ear.

When I returned
arms extended
I had to answer again

then we rolled over
back to back
and wandered off
to sleep.

HARMONIC BALANCE

IN HARMONY

This is occupied country.
Aliens have landed
but no one's listening to the radio.
Water towers are graffiti-stricken Martians
invading on tip-toe.
They spew forth hard water.
We drink and are overwhelmed.
Time soaks our rusting bodies.

The streets are windswept
passages of history.
In low-angled evening light
the storefronts are bright
as the Seven Cities of Cibola.
After school the Dog 'n Suds
is Normandy Beachhead,
the landing vehicles
filled with newly licensed
sixteen-year-olds.
Memory fails us recalling
only the past.

The retired town planner
wants to speed up traffic.
Get rid of the bottlenecks.
The streets are rerouted.
The black arrows all point
one way. No one comes back.

THE HEEBIE-JEEBIES

Twice in one day I hear it—not raven-rasp,
wind-whine, or leaf-tongue—but this:
mid-morning, sitting at a sidewalk table
next to a street where traffic comes
in exhausted phrases to the stoplight,
and our conversation spreads over
the ruin of breakfast. Wadded paper
napkins are nervous with gusts;
sides of glasses smeared with the calligraphy
of condensation; the broad-frilled umbrella
weaves a slow-moving shadow across
laps and tabletop; a waitress walks
past with a coffee pot looking for shaky
lives and finds the visitor from Alabama
leaning back in his chair, surgically describing
his illness, and how sometimes sitting alone
by a window, watching swallows sweep
past the golden-domed courthouse, the fading
sky draped in dust, silvered Venus threading
through, he gets the *heebie-jeebies*
as his skin dissolves into evening.

Tonight, the doors and windows of the house
open, the frogs and locusts loud, we can
hardly hear ourselves in bed repeat the day's
tales: meeting a rattlesnake stretched across
the driveway; the neighbor's redbone whelping
five pups in the far shed; a child who walked
off and was lost in the woods, only to be found
sleeping in his bed; and how in the garden
her skin felt oddly uplifted, more the brush
of silk along her calf and up her thigh,
an unrelenting sweet torment,

until she looked down to see her legs
moving as she stood still, skin
clouded with thousands of pin-sized
ticks racing toward her blood. It gave her
the heebie-jeebies, crawling
out of a skin not her own.

WHEN THE COWS COME HOME

Where my friend and I camped once a year,
late in the summer, was between high
pine-studded hills. It was my grandfather's
dairy farm and the herd pastured there
sometimes, but not recently enough
to crop the grass back. We cut
a wide circle and pitched a canvas tent.

Nights were already chilly and I decided
to collect firewood along the edge
of the field. My friend stayed in the tent
to arrange the food, flashlights, axe,
water bottles, and whatever else
we hauled from the house.

From the pines, I saw a Holstein herd,
twelve cows, plodding toward the pond,
the tent directly in their path.
I dropped the wood and ran,
but they'd already reached the clearing.
Bovine curiosity had lined them up,

shoulder to shoulder, crowding together,
packing-in their thick, curly heads to stare
into the odd opening, their wide eyes
swimming behind black and white snouts,
hardly smart enough to ask the question
to the answer they found.

My friend, a dedicated coward, trapped
in the tent, pressed against the back wall,
lunged for the pistol loaded with blanks
and fired wildly. The cows, too close together
to turn around, too stunned to run forward,
too shocked to back up, and wedged together

by their fear, rose in unison on awkward
hind legs, their front hooves galloping
in the air, udders indecently exposed,
a chorus line of herbivores, and as if on cue
they emptied themselves of an afternoon's
grazings, covering the entire circle

of cut grass, the tent inside and out,
sleeping bags, firewood. After bowing
to their own abundance, they came down running
away from a world that had suffered a mammoth
overripe hemorrhage and back to the barn
where they didn't give milk for days.

TRUCKING CONFESSIONS

I don't control the weather. At three in the morning, I have only one or two things on my mind, and that's mostly just get there. Get there on time, get there and stop the passing neon smear through the side window that stretches across every city, get there and forget straight ahead, get there and remember to lie still and not swing at the first sideswiping remark.

Like I said what could I do. I'd seen enough deer edging the gravel shoulders, dead and alive, rotting and grazing, that I had one foot on the brake, ready for the sprinting phantom crossing the two-lane. Eighteen wheels and eighteen gears, fifty-six feet of hurtling metal, CB static and radio talk shows preaching the Lord, apocalypse, welfare queens, secret governments, and alien corpses in cold storage, all aswirl in my horse-head-high, headed-for-the-stars cab, though I could hardly see more than a hundred feet ahead through sleet mixed with snow and night.

It's movie magic the way headlights pick up each dazzling flake and streak it toward the windshield, as if I'm the only target of the universe. Like I said the road conditions belong to the road, I just have to get through, and as you know, on that bend in the poverty of backwoods and mountains in the southern reaches of this state, where the road conspires to tie itself up and send us back where we came from, ice caught the wheels of the trailer and sent it swinging across the median, folding up behind me, a jackknife.

I'm this giant metal blade sweeping through the dark, tires churning gravel, plowing half-frozen dirt, the steering wheel setting its own course, storm-beached diesel leviathan, and the van coming from the other direction is mangled, minced, cut-in-half, flipped, and by the time I've returned to time and a heart-pounding stillness, lights from north and south have flared from stopped cars.

In the paperweight silence of spinning flakes, there's a family, five out of six, who once knew something of this night, who had a bet on a destination and found it here in these sagging pines, who knew of others who will keep waiting even after the phone call. What could I do? What else could I do? I've got to get some sleep. The road keeps jack-knifing in front of me.

ALWAYS MENTION A GUN

At an intersection on Cherokee Avenue,
a woman holds up a cigarette as she staggers
out of the dark. She might be asking
for a light. The car windows are closed
so we can't understand. We don't want to
according to the man sitting next to me.
He says a light leads to spare change,
to drugs, to offers of sex, to pleas for a child
sleeping wrapped in a blanket in a doorway.
Forget all the details, simply say a light leads
to death, and tonight we believe in something else.

We are headed to the Way Out Cafe
for a late night where anger is beat out
in words on a stage, wounds freshly
wrapped in syllables, loss everything
that is finally summed and shouted
over the shaved heads and dyed hair,
over the pierced noses, eyebrows,
over the blue swirl of tattooed shoulders,
leather and jeans, through clouds
of backlit smoke that plunges acrobatically
into the exhaust fan, until there is no one
left to face the microphone.

Afterwards we see a car perpendicular
to traffic, half in the street, half in the park grass,
doors open. We follow Iris, Magnolia,
Flora, to his turn-of-the-century house.
He says in this neighborhood,
there's *zero tolerance*. They call the police
on anyone who's suspicious. To get a response,
he always mentions a gun.
Since I will be up late reading,
he shows me how to set the motion
detector. The numbers are easy to
remember, 1-9-7-6, the Bicentennial.

At the second floor bedroom window,
I see a steetlight wreathed in mist,
the white-capped sheen of a cobblestone sea,
the wet shadows of avenue trees. Too close,
I hear two shots fired from something large.
Something powerful and threatening.
The air is left ringing. Under these high
ceilings, I'm unafraid, as if I might climb
out of reach into a heaven of plaster angels
and filigree. In the morning newspapers, nothing
reported. Just two more holes in the air.

A DOG'S LIFE

It was just a damn dog.
How was I to know
it belonged to old man Meyer
a couple miles down the road?
I thought it was a stray
and when it wouldn't leave the yard,
leave our dogs alone,
and started at our chickens,
I threw a stone or two.

Damn dog still didn't run.
From the closet I pulled the shotgun,
slipped in a cartridge,
locked the barrel shut,
and fired into the air.
In the chicken coop
it looked like a snowball fight
as they hit the walls, floor, ceiling,
all at once. The dogs tore off
like a page from a girlie magazine
in the hands of a sixteen-year-old.

Well, as soon as I walked into the house
it was back digging in the yard.
This time I aimed and threw the mangled
carcass in the ravine on the other side
of the pasture for the crows
or coyotes, whoever got theirs first.

After a night in jail, lawyer's fees,
courts costs, and fine, I'm $450.00 poorer,
not to mention, everyone in town calls me
"mutt masher" or "great white hunter."
If that wasn't enough, I'm being sued
for another $26,000 in damages.
The damn mongrel didn't cost more than ten.
I got three of my own.
I'll give him one of mine.

BROTHERHOOD

Following that yellow line far into the dark,
I just passed the moon. Forget the cosmologists,
I'm driving a car with an odometer
that reads a quarter-million miles.

Proof enough for any expansive theory.
Once in awhile, there are directions,
"Tear here to open," then the mangled
and forlorn fall out. The mascara of skids

runs the length of the highway and I hardly
bat an eye. There's a few radiant rusting holes
in the rear hatch. The hood and left fender
are primed black where a deer and beer

collided late one cosmic night. Don't look inside.
The coffee-stained ceiling is morning's rushed
star chart. There's enough dust on the dash
to choke a galaxy into life, and there's a second

planet of gravel rattling over the rotting floorboards.
I'm driving, one arm out the window and up
in the air, as if I'm asking a question at sixty
miles-an-hour. Nothing but the road

to say it's my turn. It's all straight ahead
and the only answer, "Accelerate."
The sky is laid out on box springs
on the roof.   Like a theorist's missing

matter, the mattress is wedged
inside the car, bumping into
the back of my head. I lean forward,
pushed over the steering wheel. The fan

on high, heat boiling through the window,
arm out against the wind, there's no end
in sight, when the pickup, held together

with bumper stickers, trash blowing
from the bed, as if Hansel and Gretel
won't remember the way back, passes.
The bare-chested driver grins, blows
his horn, and salutes with an open beer.

HARMONY TORNADO

I was too old to believe it,
when the wind started picking up
more than candy wrappers and Coke cans.
I thought it still had a long way to go,
but I could tell it was time
to roll up the car windows
before rain soaked the seats.

I walked down the porch step,
mind you, not running,
leaving the rest of the congregation
standing under the roof.

Before I had closed the door
to the passenger side of the car,
I was face to face with a swirling demon.
I yelled but there was nothing
anybody could do.
I was sure this was maker-meeting time
as I bounced from hood to hood,
Continental to Chrysler,
tossed in the air above the poplars
that were growing beside the parking lot
(but not anymore)
then dropped in the soggy ditch
as if I wasn't good enough.

My glasses were on the lawn
of the house across the street,
my Bible next door in the rosebushes,
and my wallet two blocks away
near an overturned mailbox.
I guess you could say
I was a man about town.

When the congregation crawled out
from under the heavy oak pews

everyone was shouting miracle, miracle.
All I know is next week
when I attend the Bible Baptist Church
I'm going to pray a lot harder
and listen to the Sunday morning
weather report.

TO PUT BY

He walks to the back of the house he's lived in all his life and finds a room that he's never entered. He opens the door and feels along the wall for the light switch. How strange to work both his palms over something cold, flat, vertical, and in the pitch of darkness, extending to the infinity of corners. For a moment, he's falling upward, sideways, and down. He secures his feet to the floor and turns. Something long and thin brushes his cheek. He spins from vertigo to fear. Quickly stepping back, he swings his arm to defend himself and his hand tangles in the pull chain. A dusty bulb shrouded in cobwebs ignites, as if a clod of earth were glowing from the low ceiling.

He coughs from the musty odor of things sealed and undisturbed. From floor to ceiling, he is surrounded by shelves. On each shelf he sees old glass canning jars. Thousands of Ball jars crowded into rows and labeled, the hand-lettering faded beyond reading. He looks for pickles, peas, pears, parsnips. It's not what he finds. From the top shelf, he pulls down jars packed with cirrus, cumulus, nimbus, stratus clouds, all of them sealed tight. He sees all the faces and animals and the grotesqueries that ever came to him, lying on his back in fields staring up at the passing days: the flocks of sheep, herds of buffalo, legends of Roman soldiers, flotillas, armadas; the islands, archipelagos, continents where he wanted to spend his summers and falls; and the dancing Katchinas, the spirits that surely must be behind it all.

On the lower shelf are jars of wind. There's the one that softly dissolved him as he sat on the porch one long late afternoon. In the next, the wind that pushed waves into his boat as he crossed a lake, and the gust that caught his kite, breaking the twine, releasing him to blow across a field. The other jars are aswirl with what hasn't arrived.

There are jars of snowflakes, each classified according to its intricate frozen lattice. There are sunsets packed like colored sand in shot glasses sold in stores along the highway in Tucumcari and Yuma. Jars of light rain and mists, deluges and floods. Forty days and forty nights of jars. Jars of extinct bird songs, jars of grackle crackle and sparrow twitter, so many he can't reach, sitting too far back.

He finds the shelf full of his breathing: the very first one that burned his lungs into life, the longest one when he fell from the oak breaking his arm, all of those from the hospital waiting for his father to die, all those inhaling the fragrance of another's hair, the new jars appearing at that moment to take in the breathing of this room.

HIS BEST BARK

In plaid, red-flannel pajamas, hair wild from sleep, eyes focused on a weathered world, he stands at the railing, the wood deck sagging with age and his weight, the house behind him filled with sleepers, and before him within arm's reach ragged, gray-barked winter oaks.

He listens to the neighbor's dog run though dry leaves down the far side of the hollow and cross the creek toward him. The dog stops, starts, pauses to bark, as if doubting what it hears, then another bark. Just beyond the stacked woodpile, they both see the fox, its white-tipped tail a baton bobbing up and down, leading the forest in a predawn parade.

The dog, half pit bull, half mongrel, wants to follow the red fur. The fox bounds forward and yaps, its bark sharper, more playful. The dog answers. The fox slows. The dog draws closer. The yapping and barking goes on. How much longer before they meet? The sun a dull eye through the fog.

Growing cold, perhaps feeling left out, he grabs the railing, steadies himself, opens his mouth, head thrust slightly forward, then barks. The dog, stunned, stops, spins, runs down the hill, leaping the creek, and races back to its house before turning and barking back. The fox strolls away and up the hollow, yapping every few steps.

THE BODY OF WATER

THE COLLECTORS
for Rod Santos

This is drought, and all the sacrifices,
leaving the car windows down, the barbeque
pit open to puddle and rust, the sheets
and pillow cases hanging on the clothesline
mimicking clouds come to rest, or standing
in the yard with or without clothes, any-
thing that might draw rain down, having

given up the turtle shell rattle, the eagle
bone whistle, bare feet moving in circles,
enjoining the desiccated earth to rise
as dust around ankles, the breathing of
a prayer; and still no rain, so we walk
across what water once covered,
the hard-crust sand at the head

of an island, following the splay-toed tracks
of blue herons and the smaller sandpipers,
watching a gull fly along the distant
cottonwood crowded bank above a wing
dike, where water heaves itself forward
and is shoved back to mid-channel, but is
not enough for stranded barges and towboats

scraping their flat hulls, waiting for
dredges to scoop out the silted-up river-
bed, and then one final trip to port to ratchet
steel cables to capstans that will stretch
and snap, and drift nowhere but down.
At our feet, spreading over this end of
the island and back into the murky water,

are stones polished by the river's tireless
turning, stones rolled and tumbled toward
annihilation, stones so thin they are

nearly transparent and delicate as insect
wings, and among their vitreous shimmer
there are handfuls of petrified wood, bone
fragments, amber, the teeth of extinct bison,
arrowheads and flint chips, stones without
names that have memorized earth's ancient
cracking, their surfaces shriveled black
and lined with deep creases; this is what
the river leaves, the hard shadows of
water's withdrawing, a rain of stones.

ONE BIRD, ONE STONE

for Peter Noce

The road to the house
follows a razor-back ridge.
On either side creeks meander,
and at odd turns reflect
sheets of rippled light.
He stops the van on a wide
curve before the barn, opens
the door, jumps out without
a word to his passengers,
and runs past the century
walnut that lords over
the pasture where he was
married a second time.

A squat, balding, bespeckled
Sicilian with quartz crystal
and chert arrowhead tied to
a leather cord around his neck,
an angora rabbit vest trailing
heron and crow feathers, red
sweatband circling his head,
sandals invisible in the knee-
high grass, all making swift
and elegant moves in erratic
directions across the field.
He stops near the fence,
as if coming to the end
of one world, and dives
over the edge leaving stunned
faces in the van windows.

He reappears holding at arm's
length, upside down by its claws
and struggling, wings flapping,
beak slashing, a wild tom
turkey, whose long stiff beard
hairs he will wear the next day

hanging from his neck, like
a small broom that sweeps
as he walks a room no one
else has seen.

CHICKEN LITTLE REVISITED

I saw two men carrying
    a piece of sky under
        their arms, nothing

mythic or legendary,
    simply workers in
        baggy, paint-stained

overalls, sleeveless t-shirts
    and small white caps that
        displayed their latest

drunken brush strokes,
    as if they wore
        the solitary rooms

in which they live. The full
    length mirror reflected
        a few scattered clouds

and doubled an already
    infinite blue,
        which is only

another version of absence,
    and is one explanation,
        why their arms lay across

the glass at either end
    and pressed hard against
        their bodies, as if what

they carried was more
    fragile than anything
        about themselves,

their arms floating
    outside the sky, while
        their shadows stretched

across the sidewalk
and angled up the sun—
struck stucco wall.

THE OLD ANXIETIES

Scattered over the sidewalks of June,
acorns smaller than match heads;
shadows of leaves curling into fists,
surrendering to the lightest breeze;
rising ropes of heat and the indelible
streaks of nightcrawlers

on concrete; and fields bleached
beyond themselves, glowing long after
the sun has set; everywhere beginnings
with clearer ends; and still my son
calls to me from the middle of a pond,
where he floats half-submerged

on a half-inflated inner tube, so head
and shoulders are all that greets the heat.
I don't respond, standing on the dock, and he
shouts again. The clatter of cattail blades
fills the gaps between loud words; the sweep
of a dozen swallows tangles above his head;

and his feet continue to slowly tread, refusing
the invitation to quietly escape with nothing
but handfuls of water. Alone in the unblinking,
but shriveling eye of the pond, he tries
once more, "What's the matter, getting too old?"
I point to the far shore, where a bullfrog

the size of a boot, its head the green of scum,
its body cool as mud, has just let loose
a baritone belch different from the usual
bass rolls, and it comically leaps from side
to side toward higher ground, dragging
a writhing water snake that has bitten one

of its hind legs. I continue to point, but
he can't see what it is through the encircling
surface glare, doesn't care, and wants
to know why I am still on the dock,
as if welded to the heat, and not jumping
into uncertain waters.

FOR GOOD REASON

She insists on a midnight swim
the first weekend in October
nearest her birthday, when frogs
are tentative soloists, the hunched
banks quiet, and the water strangely

empty; and some years the ones
we can no longer separate, but fuse
into an ache, are warm, and there
is little to say, except perhaps,
once in that stillness with only

her own blood-rush rocking her
in a sanguine autism, she gasped,
as if an unexpected, though not
unwanted, hand touched her breast,
swelling her heart to make room

for another year; and beside the dim
outline of willows, and the almost
imperceptible rustle of cattails
and clothes falling around the pale
stem of her body, she stepped

through her breath and down into
the fluid darkness, toes blindly
gripping slippery clay, until deep
enough to stroke, arm over arm,
farther out, following her own

splashing echoes, striking a tinder
of stars, and the chill reflections
firing the foundations of heaven,
currents of earth, and she turned back,
not trusting what she was becoming.

DESCENDENTS

1

First one tire leaves the asphalt,
and the ditch opens and the uncut grass
waves inviting us down, but not
really caring one way or the other,

and we choose the other, the steering
wheel lurching as the tires skid
back onto the road, and the trailer
pulling the boat blindly follows

with a jolt, and our hearts that
we were so unaware of swell,
claiming more room than our bodies,
and beat against the window in their

flight; and if that wasn't enough
after crossing the one lane bridge
over Bonne Femme Creek, we swerve
missing a stopped car, its door

wide open, and the driver standing
behind it half-bent-over staring
at something lying in the gravel,
and this time the truck runs

one wheel into a water filled ditch,
spinning until we are motionless,
listing like the ship we are not,
and though we continue on, four-wheel

drive lifting us out of the mud
and off the axles, we doubt
the final miles, whether we want
to or not.

2

Where the heavy sediment-darkened
currents cut away from limestone
bluffs, away from railroad tracks
that shadow the south bank, and the stone

and earthen dikes that force it back
away from plowed fields, we sail into
a buoyant flock of migrating Caspian
terns, rising and returning to the roiled

surfaces, running their open scapel-
sharp beaks across the ever slipping
skin of water; terns turning on the arc
of one wing, feathered tops spinning

in the warp and woof of flight,
a candent concatenation whirling
around us, and once through we circle
back, eager to again enter this plumed

swirl, but blending into the riparian
light, appearing over the riotous vined
and foliaged shore, spanning the tumbled
gray riprap reaching out into the river,

a single lustrous black tern glides,
as real and beautiful as the rest.

YET OTHER WATERS
for Bobette

You could not step twice in the same river;
For others and yet other waters . . .
                                    —Heraclitus

With sand to shake from damp towels
to work out of our shoes on the porch
step, turning them upside down;

to wash out hair and scalp, the softest
folds of skin; and later to fall
from the novel, its cover slightly

curled from too much sun, and there
on the desk, not to read, but to find
no good reason to continue, seeing each

grain, each rounded edge and prismatic
center, a kaleidoscope of grit to be swept
clean and carried off . . . but then I can't

stop recalling pulling her close, wet
and naked, chilled by the tidal wind
nipples puckered, the curve of her spine

drifted with sand, and the waves breaking,
breaking... Is this what
Heraclitus meant, that we could not

step into the same body twice, whether
it is a river, ourselves, or another,
that we are not just the same slipping

away, but the sand we walk over
and carry with us, caught in our cuffs
and shoes, is forever changed,

and changes us, though love may cling
like each grain late in the day
on dunes still leaning against a winded sea.

NO MATTER HOW HARD WE TRY

The wind is really nothing:
a few overheated or undercooled spaces
hyperventilating, pushed this way
or that by a few points of pressure.
Maybe it throws around a little rain
or hail at the edges, and the swizzle
stick of lightning mixes in thunder,
and once in a while winds itself
up into a tight coil sucking up chickens
and yachts. But then we cower in the poor
sullen eye of stillness as it magnifies
and blinds us until we are pulled out
of common lives into flooding streets
amid uprooted roofs and the glassy
shadows of shattered windows. Raging
tropical bodies are named for strangers,
as if our homes, once blown apart,
are large enough to invite in all
the world's extravagant nothings.

And that is why I rushed into the house
to say there is nothing to fear, but just
the same it is the spring wind; and yet
you will return to the bay window,
where there is only the slight disturbance
of leaves on the blooming lilac, and the slow
swelling of the Russian olive trees along
the fence. Beyond the yard a couple rakes
remnants of winter's rot; the pile of leaves
swirl up, a brown smoke blowing across the street.
Now I'm sorry for the interruption,
slamming the screen door and calling from
the hallway. I think I know what you
were about to say, that it was not this wind
this day, but what is relentless and dogged,
unyielding and breathless, and worse,

a panting over dusty fields, the gouging out of waves on ponds, and the slapping of little plastic flags strung over used car lots. Every face will be blasted smooth and numb, nothing left alone and growing, and always somewhere an emptiness blowing in.

EVEN AN ENTIRE EVENING
SITTING IN LAWN CHAIRS

1

Rolling over I say, "Everything will be all right,"
barely able to find my voice, only desiring a release,
wanting to sink back into the heat and the soft
pocket of sand engulfing my body.

Some day or night she knows I will be lying,
and not even know it, but simply upstaged in
a gesture, and for that reason, she cries,
and prepares to plunge into sadness that rips

the chest, saying, "Here, take it," this one fragment
of heart not worth saving, so whatever small
grace grief might harbor is lost, and the churning

and thrashing begin.

2

Even an entire evening sitting in lawn chairs,
their aluminum legs sinking into wet sand
and our feet barely visible below the muddy
water, as if we were dissolving and no one

can follow, and only the two of us can hear
each other's whispers over the river's long
vowel, and it is not enough. Behind us
are the ripple and braided patterns of receding

water, cut into the caked and cracking sand
and mud. It's like looking at one side of a knot
unable to understand how it was tied or what is
held down, except perhaps this island that the river

takes away and gives back. Sun drops below
the far shore's cottonwoods. Are we giving it
away, or is it being taken? The river's constant
overturning of one country for another is the only

eroding generosity left.

3

She does not want to hear how the possessed
also possesses, and perhaps that is why I collect
the odd-shaped stones deposited along the shore,
the signature of some other time

in this place, worn thin and with holes,
becoming something else, and less. Held
in a moment's admiration that also annihilates,
they are dropped back into drifts and debris

or slipped into my back pocket and carried
home to be dropped between the sidewalk
and the house to dissolve in the grass

and gravel.

4

Out of a night river and water warm enough
to bathe in, we pull our feet, surprised how easy
it is to reclaim abraded passions. We climb into
the V-hulled boat to float past tree-lined

banks electrified by fireflies. Overhead the scars
of meteors begin and end and evaporate
into stars. We can declare it all washed away,

that there is nothing solid but our losses.
We search the shore for the tremble of windowed
lights casting shimmering ropes over

the dark slippage.

THE HEART OF KNOWLEDGE

1

The plastic float bobs, not in the nervous
way a minnow strips bait from the barb,
or a green perch runs with the line
after swallowing the hook, rather it sinks,
doesn't move, and must be drawn in across
the bottom in front of the spillway,
through cattails and floating debris
that waits for the next rain to wash it
over the impounded edge.

Snapper snagged and dragged up the bank
wants to return to the water with fishing line
and pole. Twice it turns for the lake and is
kicked back. The third time it bites down
on a stick and won't let go, exposing its head
to the rock that crushes it, and still
the moss-covered shell crawls toward
the water but doesn't escape.

2

In the garage at his house, he uses pliers
and hacksaw to peel away the gnarled carapace
and scaly primordial hide. Gutting the turtle,
he finds the heart beating. Disbelieving,
he cuts it out and carries it into the kitchen,
filling a glass with water and dissolving
a tablespoon of salt. He drops that small
slowly contracting fist in and sets the odd
vase on the window sill in the fading light.

3

Turtle soup is tough, hardly worth
the trouble, and when he slides the dirty
dishes into the sink he sees the heart
still thumping. He opens the refrigerator,
grabs a six-pack, and places the glass
on a shelf, watching the muscle
cramp a couple of times before
closing the door.

Whatever it is on television, he laughs
and won't remember it tomorrow,
and, after half-crushing the cans, has
almost forgotten today when the small
light below the freezer reveals mold on
the cream cheese and discloses a heart
in a glass of salted water pinching
closed another time.

NEWTON REVISITED

Gravity and motion and some thing massed
to go lower, precipitous prescription,
as when I watched a man in El Dorado
Canyon, dressed only in red silk
shorts and tennis shoes, scale
a plunging granite face higher
than any city building. His thigh muscles
finer than braided rope, each spiraling
sinew compounded by another. Ascending
he grew smaller, angelic, and sometimes
swung upside down, reaching blindly out
and up over a ragged ledge, feeling for
a finger-thin crack or feeble shelf
of heaven to grab and hold. He was half
spider climbing a fissured igneous web,
and when he reached the top, fists
of lightning punched through the bellying
clouds. The canyon became a thunderous
well as rain obscured and turned
the mountain into a vertical river.

I waited out the storm in a cave,
considered his survival near naked
on a freezing mountain, his only way
down a slippery escarpment. In the middle
of the downpour, he walked up soaked
and shivering, smiling as he told how
he was unable to see his hands knuckle in
crevices, his wrists buried in the sheering
water, as if what he was descending was
water, and carried in its current to the bottom,
stroke by falling stroke, feet kicking
in a flowing firmament, until he stepped
on grounded principles.

THE CUT

All that comes back to the softly incoherent man
in the Miami Airport, who waddles through the one way
customs gate, as if the landing was a little too soon

and he was not ready to renegotiate earth, is that
he would be happy to remain high, his seat angled back,
pillow wedged in the crack between the curved wall

and back rest, watching through the triple-paned porthole
the play of light over what must be the fields of heaven,
if not gods themselves with names like cirrus and cumulus.

Sailing the blue-altered air reminds him of his home
waters, a calm Caribbean bay, and evenings in his skiff
when he would look over the gunnel and be uncertain

whether he was falling up or rising down into the draining,
sun-stained clouds. Now he flies first class, disembarks,
and walks one oceanic step at a time, maybe all at once,

morphine the perfect cocktail, his flights within flight,
with long incisions down his thighs where the plastic-
wrapped heroin is stitched under his stretched skin,

his legs wrapped in gauze and rubber under baggy
cotton pants. Perhaps too many corners were cut
so he can't think clearly in the glory and delirium-

heated onset of infection, so he pulls
at the petals of paradise as it blooms in his head,
pariah in his own promised land.

JELLYFISH

I could say these are tidal winds,
though there is not a hint of salted
air or the rotting wreckage that frames
a sea's vast litter: translucent vertebrae
and braided kelp, detritus of shells no
longer able to claim a name, flocks of
gulls scraping the scales of waves clean,
the myriad deaths the sea invents.

The clouds sweep past so thinly,
they trail the long arms of nearly
invisible creatures that can only stand
buried in seawater, barely more than
the outlines of water, and sometimes
are crushed in thousands on beaches
nonexistent as this one, leaving
gelatinous puddles that sting bare feet.

This pain could substitute for what is
screwed into skulls in emergency rooms,
on those who took a step beyond
where the stone ledge ended or missed
a turn where the road refused
their directions, and now with broken
necks they must lie awake under
an antiseptic glare, and feel it all,
each howling nerve, the spewing pain,
the screaming lack of connection,
stranded jellyfish on linen beaches.

RIVER OF DOORS

1

This is what the boy, dressed in an unzipped light-
green jacket, thought, if he thought anything at all
beyond the gesture of his last drink from an upraised
bottle, head tilted back in an exaggeration of completion,
and once drained, and without a second thought,
threw the bottle into what must have been annoying
or boring to him, that endless shattering of a seamless
flow crossing the low-water bridge, a bed of concrete
firming up the shifting gravel and sand. The bottle
did nothing of what he expected from an empty
vessel, sinking without a splash, without even its
own sucking sound or a hint of bouyancy. He quickly
turned away not wanting to watch.

2

It happens too quickly to be certain of details:
the wind catches an unlatched door and slams it
so it twists off its hinges and the glass breaks;
or the high school student, right after the morning bell
rings, walks through the full-length glass pane between
the glass doors, or in class someone else turns
to a window and begins beating her own head
against the pane, as if tired of only seeing through;
and that's how the two children fall into the river,
the rottweiler and toy collie barking from the truck,
parents scrambling down the bank, his Harley tattoos
racing along his pumping arms, her stretch pants
thumping with bulges, and they both jump into
the icy current, each one grabbing a floundering
body. What they pull up are small faces gasping
like fish out of water, and then the wailing starts,
each child clinging tightly, and the boy crying,
"I drowned, Daddy, I drowned," all the way back to
the parking lot, as if he doesn't believe he can swim
through the river's glassy doors.

THE APOSTLES

1   Jack's Not Here

Gulls gather to squawk, to fight for torn pieces of bread,
and then to complain for more. They watch closely
the angle of our bodies and hand's trajectory for any sign

of generosity. They circle over the waves and rewalk
the sand to find their oversights, and overcoming
their doubts waddle closer. The whole loaf consumed

by our profligate throwing, we leave their attention
behind and stroll the lake's winded edge. All of eleven
she races ahead, inventing a game; stick writing in

the sand the names of everyone important and distant,
and quickly remembered. She scratches a granular
side-slipping alphabet, and after each name, she runs,

as if she must catch sight of who it is. Twice I reach
her before she's finished with another cat, a parent,
or even a brother's name. The game is that she must

be done before I grab the stick and erase it with a swipe of
my foot. Sand splashes around her sprinting–
she's off, knowing who inherits the last word.

Tired of laughing and losing, I jog ahead, shirtless,
barefoot. I pass moats and towered castles already
the ruins of summer vacations; children flying

kites out over the water; families weighing in on towels.
Last summer on this stretch of beach, I saw the back of
a man's head, his hair cut shorter, newly shaved, a face

I hardly recognized, yet knew. He was standing knee-
deep in the lake throwing a ball. We each travelled
a thousand miles to arrive at these new sunburnt selves

that would fade and peel, and must soon be given back.
We smiled, exchanged our brief amazement, and parted,
embarrassed by our heartfelt emptiness. Today I reach

the iron-stained sandstone where the beach falters
and stumbles upward into cliffs, and this time he's not
here. I jog back to where my daughter is writing another

name, and dive into the cold incoming waves,
scattering the paddling gulls that would devour us
if we didn't keep moving.

2   Boundaries Pour Forth

It's never quite finished, at least that's what I think,
after listening for a week to the waves' steady voice,
when they do not bother to climb the wet ladder of

their reaching, but fall on the shore's first rung and slide
back frivolous and satisfied. What happens next is
where we, husband and wife, pick up after the teenagers

head for the beach. We sit undressed in the tent, noticing
each other's solar borders, zones crossed by hunger and greed,
but this time our pale selves surrender without terms,

and we fall deep into waves. Later in the afternoon on
hot sand, we are rubbed raw by light and are unable to touch,
but having touched dearly the lake's clear currents tighten

into a piercing blue as the sky softens, as if to accept whatever
we call it, and it is all praise, and pours forth, the tide not
ending anywhere, but taking the whole beach.

LIVING IN THE AMPHIBIOUS WORLD

. . . toward lost Amphibia's emperies.
        –Richard Wilbur

His name was Frog, behind
his back Toad, and his tonnage
squatting at the entrance
was wholly batrachian
to customers entering under
the burlesque's flashing marquee.
One step back into the street
and the fog grabbed hold, clotted
over the harbor where the splintered
fingers of wharfs reached out
toward the drowning and the sea.
Inside was another descent through
smoke and cheers, where the midway
half-circled a blazing white piano
that accompanied the slink
and sway, the hard sell
and the curvaceous slide.
In the middle of each show
the angelic piano, bench attached,
would rise on pulleys toward
the ceiling, trailing a hard rain of
strutting notes. There were nights
when whoever, down on her luck,
in need of a fix, or resigned to another
naked night, twirled a ratty boa,
spun the frilly umbrella, or stood
behind a frayed peacock fan,
and then dropped them all to ride
on the music, uttering chords
of moaning just below the cracked
plaster, the whole note of her dark
cleft singing to every upturned
eye. One night after hours
Toad lay on his back, stretched
across the piano, naked as a frog,

as the latest act squatted on him.
In one clouded moment his foot
kicked the lever that started
the motor, that pulled the cables,
that had the pulleys squeaking.
The music wasn't playing when they
were found. She was smothered between
the ceiling and a squashed Toad,
and Toad was broken by the unrelenting
force of a scorched electric motor laboring
to push the music through the roof.
Decades later, in the yuppie bar,
there's a drink called the "killer piano"
that some nights doesn't take
the music higher but only scalds
the throaty notes that beg for more.

In Oaxaca doors are being opened
and doors are closed. And others
bang on their hinges for three
nights and there isn't a breath
of breeze around. In this adobe
hacienda room leads to room
and there is still another, as if
it is rooting deeper into the hillside
above the town, above the settling day's
market of dust, of cars and donkeys
and feet passing the stalls crowded
with open sacks of beans and corn,
stacks of hand-woven rugs and blankets,
designs that are a thousand years
of the hand's memory, wire-caged
chickens and splashes of parrots,
mounds of guava and mangoes too
ripe to last under the sun's domain.

In this part of the house, away from
the plaza, sleep comes slowly, heat still
crawling up the cactus slopes, inflating
the room into a sweaty calm, when
the doors softly bang, the doors that once
opened onto a patio and now swing flatly
into a wall that holds back a shoulder
of the sliding hill. The third night he wakes,
he can't breathe, there's something heavy
on his chest. The doors are banging
as they have each night. She strikes
a match, holds up a candle, and there
inches from his chin, in front of
his crossed vision, is not a heart attack
but a frog hardly larger than his thumb,
its skin glazes green, its eyes volcanic,
two rubies burning down the dark,
two boiling drops of blood falling toward
him, and as he gasps the flame gutters out.
She feels for the wall switch. He lies
perfectly rigid. The light on and there's no
frog on him, on the floor, under the bed
tangled in the sheets, and the banging
doors that let in so much remain locked.

I'd forgotten my daughter's parent-teacher
conferences, and now at work I remember,
sitting among ghosts and angels, jailbirds
and dirty old men, all shuffling papers
and answering phones. I'm wearing a fringed
leather vest, so each move, considered
and ill-conceived, trails the wake of a hundred
beaded arm-length strands; the elegance
of each defeat clearly visible. No tie-dye,
but a straw hat and a serape aping a sunset,
along with cowboy boots bought at an Albuquerque

church yardsale, enough diamond cross-
stitching on the bootleg to shame a rattle-
snake, and toes so pointed they could thread
a needle. On the phone my daughter
threatens never to go back to school,
knowing I'm costumed for Halloween.
I go anyway. In science, snakes watch from
terrariums as I move across the empty
room to the small chair in front
of the teacher. Her desk is heaped
with coral, books to identify the furred
and feathered, startling minerals,
hooked seeds, exoskeletons, teeth
that bite the dust covering them, shells,
and fossils. I can barely see her though
our voices easily carry across the wreck
of this exhausted gesture. On the front
of the desk's gray-scratched metal skirt
a poster is taped: *Agalychnis Callidryas,*
the red-eyed tree frog, its jade skin
a hypnotic jewel glistening over
a jungle of desks, so much larger
than this life or its own.

FATHERS IN THE NEW WORLD

The news is Columbus didn't discover
anything; the world was flat
and he fell off the edge full-sailed,
his ship cutting the wake he feared,

so he folded far-known edges
of his tattered map together
and declared India, though no one
there would ever see him, leaving

terra incognita for a rainy day
when drifting was safer, queens easier
to convince, Indians sweating
into gold pieces, and ships' holds

crammed with melted gods that would
sail centuries across wet sand; and I'm left
with randomly parked police cars
across a field and a backhoe digging

around a barn for graves, food stolen
from prison kitchens and not by the inmates,
the minimum wage raised to another
minimum, and though photographs

from space show the earth rolling on,
the photographs are flat.

CALLING BACK THE HIGH HURDLERS

Moist, glandular skin, scaleless,
head and trunk fused,
seven vertebrae, grandiose vocal sacs,
webbed toes for climbing walls of water,

shortened forelegs, hind legs meant
to leap and not stop even in the frying
pan after a night's gigging.
They eat only the living,

swallowing whole what sticks to their
tongues; so unlike what rolls off ours
and stutters forth carelessly, simply getting
it said, story upon unstuck story, our strategy

a sprawling abundance, theirs hunger.
With soprano shouts and trilling screams,
with bass eruptions and not one syllable
less than many, in the vast swamp

choked with primal croaking and rasping,
their heads and bodies submerged, their eyes
just breaking the surface, they watch the snake
and heron, the kingfisher and raccoon, all desiring

their fill of amphibian dreams. But even now
they disappear, without clear explanation, beyond
predation and hibernation. They disappear beyond
their lives in both worlds, so even Aristophanes

wouldn't be able to call them back with his chorus
of *bre-ke-ke-kex, ko-ax, ko-ax*; and it's
not because a princess, who lost her golden
ball, has thrown her frog against a cold wall,

only to lose it again to a handsome stranger;
and it's not that these high hurdlers are filled
with buckshot and can't get out of Calaveras

County; or are dissected one too many times
to reconstitute another species of knowledge
and compassion–no matter what we say,
our amphibious lives are threatened
in both worlds.

MAP TO THE PARTY

If you wait, you grow old, nothing
more. Traveling light is your only
illuminating illusion.

Either way you can't remain,
time and place inseparable.
To settle is to amass names:

lespedeza, hickory, Providence Road.
To accelerate is to compress
latitude and longitude,

to shoulder wind in every
direction, to wear a hole
in the already worn cartography.

To grow old is to grasp sheer
granite faces, to negotiate
declivities and eruptions

of aspiration, to disbelieve
coded legends, to find instead
water's divides, to follow the rule

of thumb–civilization's always
down stream, a steaming ruin,
a crumbling repository, a flow,

a seepage, the final flush
to sea level and lower. Buried in
the alluvium: Etruscan bronzes,

eroding pyramids, coral-encrusted
hub caps, cracked glass fishing
floats. On an oil-blackened spit

the aging Archimedian rabble
gathers to count the grains
again, praying for a mistake.

HOUSE OF TURTLE

I can't tell you where to start, maybe I don't know,
or maybe I'm simply not ready for the responsibility,
though it has nothing to do with not wanting to help,
nothing to do with all the possible guilts that sweep

over us for not having loved enough, or been present
enough, or even not having stopped the car and moved
the turtle off the road, and finding the flattened mess
when we returned, having watched in the rearview

mirror another driver intentionally swerve. We must
take into account another time it was hopeless,
or just pointless, when we had not yet surrendered
hope, when the pond by the highway was drained

for a new apartment complex, the backhoe with its
claw sunk for the night into the breached embankment,
waiting for morning to again swallow another mouthful
of earth and spit it out. What more could be done,

the quitting-time traffic no longer able to dodge
those orphaned by the air, who crawled for other waters,
and over the asphalt the hundred or so moss-backed
shells were cracked and savaged flat. Perhaps this is

just a warning, like the children standing in a down-
pour shouting over whether running or walking
through the rain will leave them drier, even as the rain
falls harder, drenching their most refined arguments.

HIGHWAY FIFTY WEST

The engine is insistent, hungry, demanding to be fed more miles.
The windows rolled down, the long zipper of September locust
song is undone and falls into the rags of distance. In the last town

without a stop sign, light neatly folded the clapboard houses
into the envelope of long shadows. Even vultures are hungry
for the road, following it more closely than drivers, they tilt

and swivel their awkward wings low over the gravel shoulders
for what has left a humped stain. The Roman Emperor Nero commanded
Seneca to suicide, perhaps for telling him that if he wasn't happy

with what he had, which was all the known world, it wouldn't matter
if he possessed even an unknown empire. But then history's fatal
collisions are not the same and will not be remembered on this road,

but relived in the small plastic-flowered crosses by an overpass.
The scarlet rash of sumacs bleed up hillsides. The sharp blue edge
of horizon cuts above soybean fields. In the drainage ditch cattail blades

are honed on yellow shafts of afternoon, and in the turbulent wakes of
passing traffic can be heard the clatter of ancient duels, frog and snake
fattening for hibernation. The bald monuments of roadcut rock display

the scars of exposure, drilling and dynamite, and begin to glow in the full-
face of late sun. On a tarnished plaque below a statue of Columbus in a square
in Barcelona, on a similar sunny fall day, can be read the inscription: "You

have to navigate. You do not have to live." On this road that we desperately
want to disobey–it makes no difference if we suddenly wrench the steering,
swerve, hit or miss, we crash through the bronzed light of evening.

INVENTORIES OF RUIN

. . . not all of us live in the same ruins.
—Gerald Stern

1

EVEN the crooked is straight at any one
instant, when there's no forward
or going back, no sideways to consider,
just the asphalt beyond making capricious
turns. How it goes on or ends without us,
as it did Friday when night sped past
the overturned Ford that clowned
somersaults over the median, tossing
those drunk on immortality to the pavement
and ditch. There was no turning back
for them, or even for doubt in the careening.
In the wreckage of my own life, the dark
is sleek with rain, the windshield wipers
beating above the radio static, my arm around
a girl in the back seat when the car swerves
once, and again, and I push her to the floor
before I curl next to her just before the first
roll, and the rolling that goes on across
the highway. We were weightless, floating,
turning freely in the air, in a cage of shattering
glass, before skidding upside down to
a stop. We reentered the world through
a broken window into a buzzing rain.
The driver, jammed between the seat
and steering wheel, continued to drive on.

2

I don't know what to tell him, my son.
I want to tell him too much. I worry
over what he has or has not learned,
and I'm not sure which is the most
troubling, but catching myself either way.
If I tell him, he will have been told,
and I certainly don't know by telling

if I've told him enough, or if he will
think it's enough, and if he does think
it is enough, then there's little more,
which means I've told him too much,
that enough then, for him, is everything.
If I don't tell him, and he thinks
that's enough, that is, everything
I haven't told him, and he leaves
it at that, then it's never enough.
What I'm left with is that nothing
is enough. But what I really want
is to let him feel it flow through his
fingers, hands moving in ever widening
circles to catch what is lost, and lost
to catching, until there's no difference.

3

Should I mention how the next day
after the wreck I couldn't move
my left arm. X-rays revealed nothing—
adrenaline paralysis. Or how another boy
drove his car south on West Boulevard,
past houses surrounded by wide oaks
and ample lawns, accelerating past one
hundred miles per hour through
a stoplight and intersection where right
and left were the only choices,
and he chose straight into a limestone
road cut and the newspapers. Until
the road was widened years later,
each time I passed I turned to see
slivers of glass, flecks of chrome,
glitter on sunny days in the grass
and in the stratified layers of ancient
seas. Should I mention this? Have
I said too much, moving beyond
simple caution and common
sense into inventories of ruin.

BEHIND THE POWER PLANT IN THE
PARKING LOT BY THE BRUSH PILE

Rough pine-shaped flames take the whole day to sputter out.
From this angle I can't see who holds the match lighting
so much darkness, and I doubt anyone but God holds a concept of pain
with so much to burn. Later a few insomniacs hold

their hands over the heart of the glowing shadows, trying to stay warm.
I can't, or don't dare, I'm not sure which, and remain behind rolled
up windows. For now sparrows claim a majestic dead limb. The day
hobbles along through snow flurries. Is there always a reason

for the pain that burns in each of us? We accept the pointless
suffering of others; it's easier than for ourselves. The foundation
of reason is belief in reason. We believe in the goodness of pain.
Reason with its greater good is hardly more than a crushing whisper

of ash spreading in November winds. A bruised red car pulls
in; someone is later than usual, for good reason, an honorable
if not perfect loss, I'm sure. The door slams, and she rushes
off, straightening her skirt, adjusting her purse, too distracted

to notice the flaming dark around her life. She passes a mottled
gray and white pigeon, from a family of bridge sitters and eave
hoppers. It thrashes between concrete parking bumpers, one wing
unable to remember flight, or flying off by itself, dragging

along the failing body anyway. Hit by a car, or by a boy adjusting
the sight on his Christmas present, or methodically poisoned on
the steepled roof of the nearby Methodist church–we are given to
killing and killing to pray–the spastic flapping slows, the pigeon

rights itself, stumbles backward, as if to make another run at flying
into the asphalt. I watch from a car in the parking lot, surviving
loss a kind of pleasurable pain. What we remember most
and longest are the flights of fancy and the rough landings after.

REMEDIES FOR VERTIGO

from EXPERIMENTS IN FLIGHT

1. Playing Chicken

When his mother sent him to catch a chicken
strutting in the yard, he knew not to walk
directly toward any one of the flock pecking
and scratching amid the weeds and tireless cars
mounted on concrete blocks. He must act
as if he were headed in another direction,
and only coincidentally walking past
toward the shed for a shovel or to the storm cellar
for potatoes, all the time edging ever-so-slightly
sideways while staring straight ahead, but really
watching from the corner of his eye, then springing
and bending in one scooping motion into his arms,
a squawking, flapping chicken, then holding it
at arm's length by its scaly, clawed feet. It wasn't
that "eat or be eaten" wasn't clear to him,
but that he'd never wrung their necks the way
his mother had shown him; he squeezed the air out
of them, as if holding a feathered bag pipe
under his arm, their jabbing beaks turning
in a slow, dizzying motion until the last note
died away and they hung limp. He loved to show off
to passing neighbor kids, how he was old enough
to pluck the world of its terrified notes.

6. Flying on Instruments

In the flashlight's beam, he follows the frantic
flutter of a dusty brown bird up and down
the shed's cobwebbed window, leaving dusk
streaked with dust and stars. This bird, perhaps
a flycatcher, tries desperately to fly deeper into
night's glittering glass as he approaches and fails
at rescue before grabbing it with one hand
rather than scooping with two. He is surprised
by its weight, or lack of weight, and feels
uncertain how tight to hold a handful of air.
He steps from the door into the dark
and he almost doesn't notice his empty hands.

TO KEEP GOING

Far up the valley,
from deep in the willow thickets
along the creek, a bird call
comes I don't recognize.

Juan Ramón Jiménez wrote
that he would *go away,*
and the birds will still be
there singing. He was right,

he went away, and some of us
still hear him in the branches
beside our houses
and far up cold creeks.

But there are those birds
that have left too. The last
dusky seaside sparrow died
in a cage behind beach dunes

in Florida, unable to call in a mate.
The shrike, the butcher-bird, Jackie
hangman, the strangler, all names
for feathers on the same bird,

a songbird that goes against the grain
and with hooked beak breaks necks
of mice and other birds and sometimes
hangs their limp bodies on strands

of barbed wire where they dangle
like half-eaten laundry, their song
disappearing too, along with
the meadowlark that has perched on

a fencepost in my garden and tilted its
head back, stretching its neck, exposing
a black feathered necklace as it points
its bill skyward, clearly announcing

spring, a yellow-breasted soloist
fronting an orchestra of greening
grass, it too is going away, and for
no good reason that we understand,

and so there are fewer notes
to remind us of his going.

ACID RAIN

Stainless bolts slipped from his hands.
He was already balanced on air
and one breath away from his last
as it passed quickly and too easily through
the safety netting. A familiar story,

drinking hard all night, beer for breakfast
to sober up. He held tight to the ladder,
his stretched safety belt an umbilical cord
unwilling to sever into an airborne birth.
The clatter of steel woke him,

his foot slipped back onto a rung.
He watched a silver rain disappear
600 feet below him. He didn't hear
their impact, or the shouts and curses
of hard-hatted men below. They pulled out

tape measures, probed the holes
in the cinder-packed ground down to three
feet, men who liked to know to the fraction
of the inch how close they came. The men
sitting around blueprints in the company trailer,

stared through holes in the ceiling,
the ones in the floor, tell what they saw
after work on tailgates and in bars.
From the top of the power plant smokestack,
going higher to disperse the smoky truth

in exchange for the lies of light
and warmth, the man jerks his safety belt
back into place, begins threading
another bolt as he falls through
another hole in the clouds.

THE CIVILIZED SACRIFICE

I have climbed the backs of gods too. It's not so
strange, dressed in heavy coat and boots, hat
pulled down to the eyebrows, cheeks windburnt,
gloved fingers numb, and each brief breath prayed

upon, each step thrown onto the loose altar of stone.
Blinded by spires of light, I've looked away
as the unblemished blue splintered in all directions.
And I've backed away from the sheer

precipice, the infinite suddenly a fearful measure,
the way down to tundra and the jagged maze of
granite, leaving only a crevice in which to cower.
I've lain on the steep slopes of night under spruce,

wrapped against rain and cold, and watched clouds
explode in my face. Stark boughs reached
then sagged back in a sweeping, resolute silence.
I was shaken loose by thunder and lightning,

like the small girl, named Juanita by strangers.
She tumbled a hundred yards down
Nevado Ampato peak, her whereabouts unquestioned
for five hundred years until a nearby volcano

began a festering eruption, thawing the slope,
and wrapped in her *illiclia* shawl woven in the ancient
Cuzco tradition, wearing a toucan- and parrot-feathered
headdress, her frozen fetal posture a last effort

at warmth above tree line amid ice fields, there
to address and redress for rain and maize, for
full vats of fermenting beer, plentiful llama herds,
for the civilized sacrifice, to be buried alive and wait

in private, as we all do to speak with our gods, hoping
to appease, to know, to secure the illusive cosmic
machinery, and in that last numb moment her left
hand gripped her dress for the intervening centuries.

HOW HE DIED

It was years later,
maybe three, maybe five,
after he climbed the sheer
vertical granite that rose
a thousand feet above
the mountainous gravel
road and the torrent
of snowmelt flooding
the creek, near where I
stood and watched.
He wore only tennis shoes,
rosin bag, and red silk
shorts—without ropes,
only the grip of his hands
and braided muscle of
his legs. I looked away
once, at a water ouzel
pumping up and down
on a water-smoothed
boulder before it dove
and flew below the rapids.
So agile, he was nearly
to the top when I glanced
up when the canyon
detonated with thunder,
was obscured by rain,
and he continued
to climb into the clouds.

SPARROWS

They are alert to danger, life and death a score
simply kept by beaked heads bobbing up and down
among scattered seeds. They are on the small concrete
basketball court beside the house—its symmetry at odds
with a field crowded and burnished purple by stalks
of broomsedge and the shrinking geography of crusted snow.
Sparrows randomly rearrange themselves, unless hunger
is an order, flying back and forth between barbed wire
fence and buck brush. Back after a night of subzero
temperatures, there is desperation in their search,
eyeing the crouched housecat, as if it were nothing more
than a misplaced shadow shaken loose from its light,
the hungry welcoming winter's early end.

Much as the cargo planes that left the secret airfields
of Buenos Aires, decades ago, during the "Dirty War,"
that leveled off far out and high over the windswept Atlantic,
and there, which is nowhere that is known or can be found again,
students and union activists, teachers and artists,
were shoved through open doors, the whole world
their flyway as they flew into the face of their beliefs,
what they'd held onto in cold cells, strapped to tables and chairs,
against cigarette burns and electric shock, and questions
never meant to be answered. Surprised, they spiraled
down, arms and legs spread, that they could not perch
on the air, and before they could consider other possibilities,
they plunged through their wet shadows.

Charles Lindbergh, first pilot to fly solo across
the Atlantic, his plane, The Spirit of St. Louis, hangs from
the ceiling of Lambert Field Terminal, its glistening body
catching the thousand eyes of travelers rushing to the next
flight—his son also disappeared, kidnapped and killed—
he said, ". . . if I had to choose, I would rather have birds
than airplanes." Today mothers, thousands of miles
away and years later, hold up placards, wear pictures

of their sons and daughters hanging from their wrinkled
necks, the glossy photos shining in the sunlight, all that's left
as they gather each week without fail, though some have
already grown too old to ever forget or return to the Plaza de Mayo
in Buenos Aires—but they too agree with birds, with sparrows.

PHOTOGRAPHING THE WIND

All photographs are accurate.
None of them is truth.
—Richard Avedon

This is a wholly comfortable wind,
tailored and too expensive for the end
of a ragged century. Sitting on the porch,
it has us believing again. I breathe
this wind that isn't in a hurry,
isn't pushing through the crowd
of oaks to see what has fallen, isn't
banging unlatched screen doors to get in,
isn't rattling loose panes awake,
isn't scooping up newspapers and forcing
their headlines against fences; it's already
too late. We drink coffee, balance
cups on the wooden railing and forget.

The bird in the photograph has already
abandoned the air and stands
on barren ground, a lord with wings
folded, statuesque, a feathered black
granite that has dropped from an African
sky. Though the bird looms large
and too alert, it's in the background,
and on this all too clear and sunny day
we know the bird can't be blamed.
This is simply what it knows best.
Though it may have arrived a little
early, it is certain in its waiting.

The naked child, has drawn her knees up
to her chest, her forehead pressed against
years of parched ground, her forearms
stretched forward and away from either side
of her thinning body, her back to the steadfast bird,
guardian of this warring, drought-stricken plain.
This is when we want to believe in a wind

such as this one crossing the porch,
that refuses to carry a cry or spread
the scent of finality, and instead braids
strands of warmth through the cool
of evening, between the spaces of outspread
fingers, our hands failed kites,
our lives falling through this luxurious air.

ANGELIC LONGINGS

Beside the empty plates the folded wings of angels.
The scepters of knife, fork, and spoon lie on the table.
The diner's etiquette calls for feathers to be dabbed
at the corners of mouths. Lipstick and gravy trace the zenith
of flight. Wings fluttering across laps are the zeitgeist of arousal,
reason enough for these cravings. A few guests still don't understand,

become uneasy when a hand reaches under the table
to caress their angelic longings. The table cloth rich
with spilled burgundy, traces the borders of intoxicated continents
that wait to be explored by a pair of fallen tongues,
and later with the soft panting of wings. There are angels
with insulated wings that hold up the heated corners of hell

and a flaming fondue. They keep vigil by the oven door
to escort a roasted soul to the carving block. In the living room,
the crowd grows anxious. Between the sofa and the ceiling,
Saint Albert tallies four hundred million of the winged.
Kabalists wearing zircon rings agree. One wet white blur
works the four thousand nine hundred names

of God. Another is half fire, half ice. The spooked guests begin
to think angels everywhere, even converting the kitchen witch.
No matter how humble and discrete the conception,
because the guests can think of God at all, must mean there is God.
They'll argue details and style over another glass of merlot.
On the radio by the couch, it's reported

an artillery shell exploded in the crowded market
of a besieged city. Sirens sailed loudly through the air for hours.
Because men can conceive of death, they have become
its overheated engines. In the dining room no one is listening.
Saint Albert uses the Heimlich maneuver on the host
choking on a buffalo wing, her face turning angelic blue.

RED SHIFT

If you lost something red on Tuesday,
        as the sign taped to the west entrance
door asks, it must not be the Coke machine
        thrumming its one tune, change
rattling in its throat, cans rolling off
        its tongue–thirst always glowing
at the end of a long dark hallway.
        It's not the exit signs above every
door, warning us not to stay too long,
        that this way is the way out
when necessity arrives as it always does,
        but if we look down another hallway
there's a sign claiming its the way out,
        in rain, in sunshine.
It's certainly not the fire extinguisher,
        recessed into the wall, where it sits
all day behind glass, a museum of our
        incinerating fears, waiting for us
to rediscover our own or someone else's
        emergency and then to break
the glass with a fist or spiked heel
        and appear out of the smoke a hero
or in ashes. Perhaps it's a simple
        misunderstanding of how celestial
bodies travel vast hallways, not realizing
        that as we move away from each other,
the distance squares the speed squaring
        the distance, that light shifts across
the spectrum toward longer wavelengths
        and all that is left is a red glow,
what is found of your leaving,
        so even if you did lose something
red on Tuesday, as the sign asks,
        we can't call back this universe.

WEST OF WEST

MANIFEST BREAKFAST

In a house buttressed by books and slanted morning light
slicing across the grain of the kitchen table, Lieutenant Colonel
George Armstrong Custer's 1876 orders to pursue the Sioux,

Cheyenne, Sans Arcs, Blackfeet, sits beside an emptied bowl
of Grape Nuts. The document is randomly punctuated with crumbs
from half-burnt toast, difficult to read the general's elegantly looping

Nineteenth Century signature and the limits of force given Custer's command.
My wife has printed over in her typewriter-meticulous style a grocery list
of olive oil, cilantro, garlic, tortellini, supplies for this evening's company,

but not the 7th Cavalry last seen surrounded near the banks of the Little Big Horn.
There's also a lengthy paragraph to herself, notes on rehabbing
the upstairs bathroom and the rest of her destiny. She's scribbled

calculations, an attempt at reviving a diminishing bank account,
and an addendum to the Christmas card list, and it's only February.
This morning my wife sits down to rewrite Custer's orders to pursue the Sioux.

SAFETY OF SUMMER EVENINGS

On this squat adobe-lined street,
the evening-heated fragrance
of roses pools around the porch,
and we believe a little more in ourselves
with each breath.
                              The cottonwood
behind the house across the street
rises up against the fading light with its
majestic wounded filigree.
                              Neighbors
discuss the heartache of lawns, the lack
of vertical development in the clouds—
no rain—notice a luminous feather
rocking on the breeze as it floats past
their small conversation, and settles
on the burnt-out grass–
                              a memory
of flight, a bird that never arrived, both
reminders of someone who ran off
to Portland, and someone else who
took a cruise to India, and how in their
own long lives they knew, when the kids
left home and the dog died that then
they were retired.
                              On summer-long
evenings, the crescent moon passes in
and out of scalloped clouds, and in this vast
space that stretches all the way to Venus,
shining by itself over a far-silhouetted
mountain range,
                              a neighbor worries over
untrimmed rose bushes too near the house,
someone could be hiding in their fragrance.

BACK ROADS

Desert dwellers will argue all roads
are back roads, and some go so far back
they lead to alien crash sites, their emaciated
remains: ratty, feathered, elastic hides,
now stored in secret military hangars,
not to be confused with Roadrunner and Coyote's.
Yes, so far back even fission finds a safe place
to expose itself.
      Today a roadrunner, large, ground-loving
bird, that looks nothing like the cartoon character,
the one that always one-ups the wily cartoon
coyote, that looks nothing like a coyote,
unless four legs and a tail are all that's needed
to belong to that class of visionary buffoons
who survive their own and our worst catastrophes,
and then do it again, falling a thousand feet
from a cliff, stepping in front of a second
speeding truck, swallowing twice just-lit dynamite
then belching the acrid smoke of an explosion.
      It's obvious, the obsession to possess
or be destroyed. Maybe it's not what we think,
not hunger but the hunt, the challenge,
the risk. There beyond the lava beds of *Jornada
Del Muerto*, is the sun-flattened Trinity Site,
the first atom-blasted crater, still closed
to the public, where Father, Son, and Holy
Ghost were fused into a Rube Goldberg
trap that Coyote now plans for Roadrunner
some Saturday morning soon.
      We stop, to miss and not miss on the hardscrabble
road, what we see through our sun-blasted faces
reflected in the windshield, a roadrunner cutting
in front of us, rattlesnake in its beak.

THE PRICE OF PALM TREES
—for Larry Levis

The currency of palms rockets fronds
into green bursts above the city,
blades slicing the burnished evening
into finer shadows, air a brassy
silent glistening like the spider-cracked
lacquer on ancient Chinese boxes.
The warm breeze entering off the desert
comforts our breathing. We inhale lizard
and cactus, acres of stones relaxing
with the day's heat. The sharp-sheathed
trunks prop up an exotic clarity
in this vast sage-scented space.

And there is the currency of palms
planted along medians: the endless necklace of traffic
pulling tight in both directions, the breaking ruby
glitter scattering for miles, leading to tract
homes stacked on desiccated hillsides
and balanced on the edge of arroyos,
under their regal rows of rising rough bark.
Backhoed into place, roots submerged
into sand and volcanic debris, they would
convince us we are graceful in this graced life.

A friend who knew the price of paradise
is dead now, alone in his house
for days when it happened, missed
by his friends who finally found him
slumped in a chair, as if he were
recalling the palm tree that he woke to in his youth,
where a rat ascended the razor-edged bark
to a hole that it freely entered and left,
its whiskered snout catching the afternoon light,
framed by the oval darkness behind it,
as if it too had a proud lineage and only
needed a wall on which to be hung.

Each day, still drowsy from his nap,
he watched the ritual climb, yet years later
he wondered if there had really been a rat,
or even a palm, but he became certain
that the rat was the soul of that tree
framed by his screened window.

Under the vast pane of polar ice
meteorites are found hinting
of other lost and more lonely places,
where WWII fighters are excavated
250 feet below, damaged only by the massive
pressures of cold, their war frozen to perfection,
where purity of form is grandiose and mundane
as six months of daylight and darkness,
where the mummified seal and human
are stark aberrations against Locke's
snowy *tabula rasa*, and under skies now blue
as ice epoch-old palms swayed into stone,
their rats gone to bone and less.

A LOCAL IS NOT ENOUGH
—for Alan Berner

Night gathers us together under a circus
of cartwheeling stars. Behind surgical masks,

our voices wildly wasted, our tongues tired and tied
by all that is unsaid. What is confessed

is only denial. Against interstellar horizons,
contusions of tone, light year's lisp, warped rhythms,

galactic collusions, where our throats gulp
down what they can, what they can't is force fed.

We are devoured and begin our painful arias
from Tucson to the muddy banks of the Missouri River.

We are dragged across mountains of broken granite,
through cholla-choked deserts, yet our pain

consumes so much more. Swallowed as we swallow:
mile-long strands of Kansas barbed wire,

tons of Wyoming high plains gristled with sagebrush,
chased with Denver and San Francisco's bristling sky lines.

A diet of asphalt and concrete, mouthful after
mouthful, and that's the easy part.

Now the humbling, the groveling, the simpering animal,
then the sphere's mad music buried under eyelids,

aswirl in novaed synapses and starred neurons.
Before the blacking in, the blacking up, the blacking out,

comets scream past. Fingernails and teeth extracted,
cattle prods and broken broom sticks, cigarette burns

and deeper violations of darkness, our raging hearts
reconfigure a universe of missing matter.

The pain that has us confessing to having lived,
out lives us even as we unlive it.

COSMOLOGICAL GAMES
—Monument Valley/Navajo Nation

Not a line in the sand,   not a Maginot Line
    or thirty-eighth parallel,   not the line

between good and evil,   salvation and damnation,
    but a limed line   in the gamed grass—

eroding quartz and lizards,   creosote roots
    and desperate thirst,   underscored

and underneath this squared,   green-sodded desert.
    There to be   lined up, ruled,

measured: drives, goals,   penalties, crossing
    and recrossing   the scrimmage line.

Uniformed, padded bodies   banked against bodies,
    fired,   the colliding energy

of Friday night stars.   No solitary Big Bang,
    but the ruled universe   of chaos, simply one

random number waged   against another
    down field. Scoreboard,   yellow and winded,

in the long game   of fragrant heat.
    Narcoleptic sagebrush   subsumes

memory, no willed   remembering. Nothing else
    happening   on Friday evening.

The applause of buttes,   cheers of mesas,
    deafening   beyond belief.

COWBOY BUDDHA
—Eureka/NV

Striped, numbered,   he's up to his old tricks.
  Last night he roped a bottle, emptied it himself.

He roped a parking meter and started shouting,
  holding on for dear life   as time expired.

He dropped the lariat   as the police passed,
  one eye in his direction, one eye on the arresting
street.

He roped a lamppost   with all the June bugs
  and mosquitoes buzzing around its flickering glow,

even a diving night hawk. Didn't lose a one
  in that late night round up. Then it was a clapboard

house at the edge of town, but it bucked loose,
  woke the sleepers inside. He'd already left

chasing another rodeo dream. Roped by his own
  thirst, he rolled up the road and began pulling

in the drought-stricken hills, squeezing out
  a last sweet drop.   Rope-braided circle

within circle playing out. One hand to the other,
  he jumps through   the ever-widening.

5:46 FREIGHT
—Tucumcari / NM

It doesn't matter,
    someone's leaving town

The streets suddenly too big,
    into junk-riddled desert,

shingle-sided houses,
    drifting like sand

Or the streets are
    each ending

no matter the direction
    anyone backs away,

of the pigeon-stained
    forgotten founder

of Guadeloupe.
    the wrong reasons,

the right ones,
    The train's sweet blur

even the parking posts
    by the station

the good, the bad, the indifferent,
    in a blur.

running out
    dead end

friends found
    crowding gutters.

too small,
    in the same spot,

or how many times
    there in front

statue of some
    or the Virgin

Leaving for all
    which are always

no matter what's said.
    so convincing

blocking traffic
    are leaning away.

ICE BOUND
—for Kale Rose

Sky's gray sheet spreads icy rain.
Through the night we heard the branches cracking.
Now they bend with the bowed ache of apostrophes.
Backs to the window, sitting on the couch, we listen
as the radio announces the list of schools closed.

An hour earlier I inched my way along
the road, tires spinning toward the ditch.
Now I read aloud to a teenage daughter,
who tolerates my foolishness, my claim
that Lao Tzu traversed a more slippery world.

With two books open on my lap, one in my hand,
two on the floor, I'm surrounded by imperfect
translations: *a gathering chaos; something*
mysteriously formed; without beginning,
without end; formless and perfect.

She responds, *Sure,*
I knew that, so what? I persist:
that existed before the heavens and the earth;
before the universe was born. She's ready to go
upstairs and listen to the radio. I ask,

What was her face before her parents were born?
she answers, *Nothing.* I ask again.
She says it again. Where are the angels,
nights on humble knees, the psalms of faith,
the saints of daylight? She walks out of the room.

I'm surrounded by thin books.
How pointless to go anywhere on this day,
or maybe any other, but then
the time comes when there is
no other way but to stand firm on ice.

CALCULATIONS

There's no turning back, every street corner is crowded with the stares
of people who haven't eaten in two days. Two days added
to two days to two days. Their clothes fall loosely.
Their drab coats and gloves wrinkle deeper than skin and clothe
someone else's body, someone with the same name and eyes,

the same lips, that speak the same words. They are restless
for no reason and turn their heads in unison looking up the street
to what could be rifle shots and down the street to what could be
rifle shots, or upward into a cloud-shredded sky to what could be wind
knifed by silence. They shift from foot to foot, lighting each other's cigarettes.

They travel whole days on these street corners and aren't surprised
to find themselves back where they started. Each evening the tales
of their travels grow longer and more exotic. In these cold March winds,
their thin clothes billow, making room, inviting someone else
to enter and live their own thin lives. Down the alley, the dull

impact of hammers. Crowbars wrench free the roof, the rafters,
the railings. They pry loose the voices of nails and wood.
They are roughly handled by numb, unwashed hands. The dirt,
the ragged calluses, the thickened knuckles, the dried blood of a dozen
small encounters are the gloves of these hands. By the empty corner store,

warming their fingers over the flames of old rhetoric, they all know
their parts by heart and hate. There's a man with a limp,
stepping into that half of the world that keeps falling away. The woman
closest holds out her one hand, the flames of buildings never felt better.
It's rumored that all the feet and eyes and hands and fingers and legs

and faces gather each evening at the edge of the city to stamp and stare
and clap and cheer even the weak endings of these street corner players
who continue to memorize the missing. The mathematics of this city
are impeccable. For the only remaining doctor, every two legs amputated
is equal to one child born. In the doorless room where the bodies

re stacked, the snow has still not melted off their boots. It's surprising,
the well-heeled have not walked off except there are not enough feet left.
The doctor pulls out his notepad and calculates. This city has never been
more destroyed and has never been more beautiful. The doctor recalculates
the weight of lost souls and predicts the city will be heavenly this spring.

VACATION AT THE END OF THE WORLD

Each afternoon the wind rushes in with its frayed brooms,
broken dustpans, sweeping up the detritus of street life
only to let it fall back into place. Heat works hard

to boil away the diluted, the excess, and the essence.
On the shore souls burn pure and clean, pilot lights for
the world's ovens. Picnic tables and lawn chairs are

what's left and even their hollow metal begins to glow
and float above the beach between walls of blue flames.
The wind rattles the cottonwood and thousands

of leaves paddle frantically, sinking into an ashen light.
The tree shimmers with the clatter of dry rain and the sand
around its trunk rolls out the glare of its thirst. There is

the hiss of fire without smoke among the branches.
Tanned skin grafted along bare backs and stretched
over oiled bellies crawls, sends shivers through the scorched,

sprawled, sleeping bodies. The lake wakes to the wind,
waves grow confused and begin to collide in white lisps.
The sopping clamor alerts the sunbathers who were

forgetting themselves and about to leave only exalted
shadows. They sit up dazed, hearing wind and rain
and fire all falling at once on their ample beach towels.

Walter Bargen has published twelve books of poetry and two chapbooks. His poems have recently appeared in the *Beloit Poetry Journal, Poetry East, Seattle Review,* and *New Letters.* He has won the William Rockhill Nelson Award, the Chester H. Jones Foundation prize, the *Quarter After Eight* prize, and a National Endowment for the Art Fellowship. In 2008, he was appointed the first poet laureate of Missouri. His website is www.walterbargen.com. He lives in Ashland, Missouri, with his wife, Bobette, twenty cats, and one dog.

Mike Sleadd chairs the Columbia College Art Department where he teaches graphic design and illustration. He has illustrated several of Walter Bargen's books. His website is www.mikesleadd.com. Mike lives in Columbia, Missouri, with his wife, Barbara, three cats, a Pyrenees, and a 200-pound Mastiff.